"*Look What God Is Doing!* is a must-read. The word that comes to mind is *power*—God's power unto salvation. When I came to chapter 2, I began to laugh with delight at how God showed up against all the forces of evil. The staging of His power was so magnificent that it literally brought me to my knees in worship. As God says in Isaiah, 'There is none like Me.' What a faith-builder! You will see the power of prayer, fasting and the Word of God, and be motivated biblically to 'hasten Jesus' coming' by getting the Gospel to every home."

—Kay Arthur, co-CEO, Precept Ministries International

"Dick Eastman's book *Look What God Is Doing!* is a must-read for every Christian, but especially leaders. His statistics alone overwhelmed me and brought me to sincere intercession. I have been deeply moved by few books, but this one is at the top of my list."

—Henry Blackaby, founder and president emeritus,
Blackaby Ministries International

"There are, as we all know, only two things on earth that are eternal—God's Word and man's soul. We need to dedicate our lives to those things that are eternal. I don't know of any ministry I have been involved with that is doing this better than Every Home for Christ. As you read *Look What God Is Doing!* you will understand why."

—David Green, founder and president,
Hobby Lobby Stores, Inc.

"Dick Eastman has had a significant role in helping fulfill the Great Commission. His commitment to spread the Gospel is an inspiration to me and to Campus Crusade for Christ. His personal involvement in teaching and documenting God's great work around the world is an amazing service to the Body of Christ. It challenges us to join God in sharing the greatest news ever. I am so grateful for Dick and Every Home for Christ."

—Steve Douglass, president and chairman of the board,
Campus Crusade for Christ International

"I have seen Dick Eastman weep over the untold millions yet to know Jesus, but I have also seen him rejoice over that one soul who has turned to Christ. *Look What God Is Doing!* chronicles the astonishing journey of Every Home for Christ, its anointed leader and those who lock arms with him for the Kingdom's sake. You will be amazed."

—H. B. London Jr., vice president,
pastoral ministries, Focus on the Family

"Jesus Himself commands us to 'go into all the world and preach the Good News to everyone. Anyone who believes and is baptized will be saved' (Mark 16:15–16, NLT). How is this possible? Well, Dick Eastman and Every Home for Christ have found the way, and we can all take part in it. And just as Mark records, 'The disciples went everywhere and preached, and the Lord worked through them, confirming what they said by many miraculous signs' (verse 20). Read and get excited!"

—Pat Boone, entertainer

"Over the past thirty years I suppose I've been in hundreds of conversations with Dick Eastman, and I have yet to come away from one without saying to myself, based on Dick's most recent reports, *Look what God is doing!* Every chapter here—so vivid, so enthralling, so memorable, so motivating—almost feels like a PowerPoint presentation on the worldwide advance of Christ's Kingdom. And best of all, as Dick points out at the outset, these stories reveal to readers in remarkable ways more of the glories of the Triune God."

—David Bryant, www.ProclaimHope.com

"Jesus was the master storyteller, using stories to communicate clearly the truth of God. Dick Eastman has followed in his Master's footsteps, using stories to demonstrate the ongoing power of God's Word to change lives. You will be thrilled and inspired as you read the stories in *Look What God Is Doing!*"

—David Butts, chairman,
America's National Prayer Committee

"Dick Eastman believes that the Lord is moving powerfully and historically these days. If you have not observed that taking place in today's world, your perspective could be radically changed by reading the exciting accounts in this book. It wonderfully personifies the heart of Dick Eastman and the incredible ministry of Every Home for Christ around the world."

—Paul Cedar, chair and CEO, Mission America Coalition

"Dick Eastman's passion to win the lost is contagious. He believes, and I do, too, that the Great Commission will be completed in our lifetime. Dick backs up his faith with the powerful testimonies found in this book. Truly God's Spirit is moving among the nations. May each testimony in this inspiring book bear fruit ten thousand times ten thousand, for the glory of God in Christ."

—Francis Frangipane, bestselling author;
overseeing pastor, River of Life Ministries

"The stories here are true and truly thrilling! Dick Eastman always makes practical possibilities out of apparently giant obstacles."

—Jack Hayford, founding pastor,
The Church On The Way, Van Nuys, Calif.;
chancellor, The King's College and Seminary, Los Angeles

"*Look what God is doing!* It's not possible to remain unmoved by the wonder-filled stories in Dick Eastman's book. God is on the move, and so are His courageous servants who brave unspeakable dangers to bring good news to those who have never heard."

—Dean Jones, actor

"*Look What God Is Doing!* powerfully documents with edge-of-the-seat intensity and well-researched clarity the remarkable transforming power of the Gospel in every corner of the earth. Dick Eastman convinces the reader that this generation could well be the generation that finishes Christ's grand assignment to reach all the world, quite literally, with His Good News."

—R. T. Kendall, senior minister (retired),
Westminster Chapel, London; bestselling author

"Required reading for every student of the Bible who prays for the evangelization of the world. This book is filled with inspiring accounts and testimonies of the Body of Christ cooperating to see mass conversions during the close of this age."

—Bill McCartney,
founder and chairman, The Road to Jerusalem;
founder and former president, Promise Keepers

"Dick Eastman's book, *Look What God Is Doing!* has ignited our souls. On every page Dick chronicles miraculous God-encounters men and women are having as a result of reading the Gospel literature presented to them by Every Home for Christ. You'll laugh, you'll cry and you'll be transformed and challenged by this new book.

We have known and loved Dick for two decades. Whether he is in a personal or a public setting, his burden for the lost is contagious. In this book Dick proves statistically that completing the Great Commission is possible in our lifetime. He challenges us to never give up reaching people for Jesus. We've read many good books, but *Look What God Is Doing!* is a great book. Don't miss falling in love with the unreached peoples of the world."

—Eddie and Alice Smith,
co-founders, U.S. Prayer Center, Houston

"To read *Look What God Is Doing!* is like reading the book of Acts today. Few ministries on earth combine a passion for prayer with a practical ingathering of the harvest as does Every Home for Christ. Dick's inspiring accounts of signs and wonders in the harvest will encourage every reader to believe this generation could well be the generation that completes the supreme assignment Jesus gave His followers—to reach all the world, literally, with His Good News."

—Mike Bickle, director,
International House of Prayer, Kansas City

Look What
God Is Doing!

Look What God Is Doing!

*True Stories of People Around the World
Changed by the Gospel*

Dick Eastman

Chosen
a division of Baker Publishing Group
Grand Rapids, Michigan

© 1997, 2009 by Dick Eastman

Published by Chosen Books
a division of Baker Publishing Group
P.O. Box 6287, Grand Rapids, MI 49516-6287
www.chosenbooks.com

Revised and abridged edition published 2009

Original edition published in 1997 under the title *Beyond Imagination*

Printed in the United States of America

Library of Congress Cataloging-in-Publication Data
Eastman, Dick.
    Look what God is doing! : true stories of people around the world changed by the Gospel / Dick Eastman. — Rev. and abridged ed.
       p.   cm.
    Includes bibliographical references and index.
    ISBN 978-0-8007-9474-3 (pbk.)
    1. Great Commission (Bible). 2. Evangelistic work. I. Title.
BV2074.E27 2009
266—dc22   2009021588

Photographs on the front cover courtesy of: Dave Hiebert, Canada (African woman); Jon Ng, Malaysia (Asian woman); and M. Nota, Netherlands (South American girl).

Contents

Introduction

On the Move

Be silent before the LORD, all humanity, for he is springing into action from his holy dwelling.

Zechariah 2:13, NLT

Make no mistake about it—God is moving by His Spirit globally in ways none of us could have comprehended even a decade or two ago.

I write this introduction having just returned from my fourth trip to Asia in the last five months. The most recent journey included an encouraging visit to Nepal where our ministry, Every Home for Christ, was celebrating its 25th anniversary of activity in this Hindu kingdom located in the shadows of Mount Everest.

Because our ministry seeks to mobilize a nation's churches to take a printed Gospel message of salvation in Christ to every home in that nation, I am always interested in the results of these campaigns. Can lasting fruit really come from so simple a strategy?

I learned that in Nepal alone, over twelve million printed Gospel messages have been "planted" home to home in the last two-and-a-half decades and more than 335,000 decision/response cards have been mailed to our Nepal office requesting follow-up Bible lessons.

What especially moved me is that our Nepal EHC office in Kathmandu now has a list of graduates of the four-part Bible correspondence course from over 9,000 different villages. This means there is at least one light shining for Jesus in 9,000 villages in that Hindu land. Further, more than 8,400 groups of new believers (called Christ Groups) have been formed in Nepal where followers of Jesus can grow and be discipled in their walk with Jesus.

I highlight Nepal because I have just observed this miracle firsthand, yet the same story could be told for regions throughout the world.

It is all part of a sweeping global revival and an accelerating harvest of souls, marked by amazing signs and wonders, that I trust will inspire you to believe that the Great Commission may well be accomplished in our generation—quite literally.

Many of the unusual testimonies shared on the pages that follow are the result of dedicated foot soldiers, both full-time and volunteer, who participate in the global ministry of Every Home for Christ (now in its 62nd year) to take the Good News of Jesus to every family in every village, town and city on earth.

In writing these accounts, I have sought to verify every testimony possible. In the twelve months prior to the original publication of this book, for example, I traveled at least eight times around the world to speak with eyewitnesses to these reports or with people who were in direct contact with eyewitnesses. Some were flown to Every Home for Christ's international headquarters in Colorado Springs, Colorado, for extensive interviews.

In several instances pseudonyms have been given to individuals to protect their continuing work in certain dangerous areas or for a more readable narrative. (The latter technique has been used in a few places when eyewitnesses did not know the names of those involved.)

While researching for this book, I also traveled both to the rainforests of the Pygmies mentioned in chapters two and three and to the mountain peoples of the Solomon Islands to see firsthand the fruit of the brave evangelists with "beautiful feet" (see Isaiah 52:7; Romans 10:15) who helped take the Good News of Jesus to these previously unreached peoples.

God is, indeed, on the move. Eugene Peterson's interpretation of the Bible, *The Message*, uniquely paraphrases the passage I cited above: "Quiet, everyone! Shh! Silence before GOD. Something's afoot in his holy house. He's on the move!" (Zechariah 2:13, MESSAGE).

Don't miss this heaven-sent move of God—and don't miss being involved in the growing global harvest that is transforming people everywhere. The pages that follow are meant to inform, inspire and even involve you in this extraordinary harvest.

When I speak publicly these days, I often begin my messages with a twofold question: First, I ask, "How many here are on your way to heaven?" Of course, in any healthy church almost everyone raises his or her hand. Next I ask, "How many want to take a lot of people with you?" The majority raise their hands excitedly again.

My motive, of course, is to challenge listeners to accept the fact that each of us has our own special harvest somewhere in the world. We need to identify it, sow into it and then prayerfully help gather it into Christ's Kingdom. We are all called to be harvest gatherers!

God is indeed springing into action throughout planet Earth and we need to spring into action with Him. Together let's gather our personal harvests and bring them joyfully to Jesus. The pages that follow will help show you how.

—Dr. Dick Eastman
International President,
Every Home for Christ

God has rolled up his sleeves.

All the nations can see his holy, muscled arm.

Everyone, from one end of the earth to the other,

sees him at work, doing his salvation work.

Isaiah 52:10, MESSAGE

1
The Sleeves of God

Sanji Adonga clutched his bag of Gospel messages tightly and proceeded to the next apartment in the central district of Yan (not its real name), a sprawling Muslim city in North Africa. Few Christian workers labored in this city of more than a million Muslims, but Sanji had an assignment from God. He was part of a tiny army of believers from a ministry called Every Home for Christ who were committed to visiting every dwelling in this North African Muslim enclave.

It had not been the best of days; most people who appeared at their doors had refused even to accept the message. But when they closed their doors, Sanji usually put a booklet on the front step anyway, so these individuals would not be missed in the house-to-house evangelism campaign. And if no one answered his knock, the young evangelist slipped the Good News about Jesus under the door. Sanji wanted every Muslim to meet Jesus. After all, he himself was a Muslim who had found Jesus.

Now Sanji was approaching the next Muslim apartment. Knocking tentatively on the door, the worker was greeted by a man in his mid-twenties. Sanji smiled and handed him the message.

"I give you the truth," he declared boldly, handing the young man a Gospel booklet.

The man took the booklet, glanced at it briefly and opened it. Then, apparently seeing a reference to Jesus Christ, he began cursing and ripped the booklet into pieces.

"This is not truth!" he shouted. "This is a lie!" With that he threw the torn booklet into the face of the evangelist. "Leave now—and don't ever return or I'll kill you!"

Shaken, Sanji headed hastily for the next apartment just up the street, and continued his work until early evening.

A Voice in the Night

The man at the door was 25-year-old Abdulai Masa, the son of a wealthy local merchant. He helped direct one of his father's businesses.

That night Abdulai fell into a deep sleep. He had forgotten the experience with the evangelist earlier that day. But during the night the young Muslim felt two powerful hands grab his shoulders in the darkness and begin to shake him violently. Was it a dreadful dream or was it real? At first he was not sure. The hands gripped tighter and Abdulai, convinced that a thief had broken into his apartment, swung his arms wildly to fend off the unseen intruder. But in the darkness he could feel no body to go with the hands grabbing his shoulders.

Abdulai's heart was beating like a loud African log drum, and he sat up shaking.

"Who are you?" he shouted. "What do you want?"

He reached up and turned on the lamp hanging over his bed. The room was empty. Still shaking, he lit a cigarette, hoping it would calm his nerves.

"Who are you?" Abdulai asked again, thinking perhaps this had been just a dream after all.

A voice filled the room.

"You have torn up the truth," the voice said with authority. Abdulai's eyes darted in every direction. Obviously another person was in the room with him.

"Where are you?" he shouted again. "What do you want?"

"You have torn up the truth," the voice repeated. "The message you were given by the visitor at your door was God's truth that points to eternal life. It tells of the only way to lasting peace and happiness, and you have torn it up."

Abdulai was still shaking. "But what can I do now? Surely the pieces of paper have been blown away by the wind."

"I will tell you where you may find another booklet. Take paper and pencil and write this address."

Abdulai could not believe he was hearing a voice with no visible body. But he grabbed a paper and pencil and wrote down the name and address of Sanji Adonga.

"If you want another booklet," repeated the voice, "you must go to this address when the sun rises. You will find the same man who stood at your door today."

Abdulai Masa slept little the remainder of the night. At the crack of dawn he dressed and headed for the address on the paper.

Sanji had just risen when he heard a knock at his door. Wiping sleep from his eyes, he opened the door and stood in disbelief as he looked into the face of the young man who had threatened his life the day before. How had this man found his address in a city of more than a million? He was certain no one had followed him the previous evening, and the only address on the booklet was a postal box in a distant city. Besides, this man had torn up his booklet.

"What are you doing here?" Sanji asked, swallowing hard.

"I've come for another booklet," Abdulai answered. "I must have a new copy of what you gave me yesterday."

"But you threw it in my face. And how did you find my address?"

"The voice in the night," the Muslim explained, describing how the hands had shaken him awake and the voice had said he had torn up the truth.

"The voice gave me your address," Abdulai concluded. "It also told me you would give me another booklet."

An amazed Sanji retreated to his bedroom and returned with a booklet. Then, for more than an hour, he used the pamphlet to explain in depth what it meant to receive Christ as Lord. By the end of the explanation, Abdulai was convinced the message was true. He repeated the sinner's prayer and gave his life to Jesus.

When he announced his conversion to his family, Abdulai, who had already changed his name to Abraham, was fired from his father's business and banned from all family contact. His father even organized a plan to have him kidnapped and killed, but one of his sisters told him details of the plan. So Abraham fled to the only Christian he knew, Sanji Adonga, who helped him escape three hundred miles south, to a less hostile area where the national office of Every Home for Christ was located.

Abraham was grateful Sanji had helped him escape, because only a few weeks later another Muslim who had found Christ in the same door-to-door outreach, the teenage son of an emir (a top Muslim leader), was bludgeoned to death by the emir himself on the grounds of his palace. The youth's entire family, as well as palace personnel, looked on as he refused to deny that Jesus was the only Son of God and was slain brutally by his own father.

But Abraham arrived safely at the EHC office to be nurtured and discipled by the director himself, even living for a time in his home. Soon he was doing odd jobs around the office and, in a few months, he began going out and witnessing house to house, telling others what Jesus had done in his life.

Now Abraham has finished an intensive Bible course and has become involved in house-to-house evangelism in regions of his nation that are heavily Muslim.

An Age of Wonders

These kinds of experiences—being instructed by a voice in the night, for example—are, as remarkable as it sounds, dramatically increasing on a global scale. God clearly has something up His sleeves, and we would do well to remember—putting aside any theology of how God might dress (see Psalm 104:1–2)—that *God has really big sleeves!* And one thing appears certain: The exploding global prayer movement is clearly related to what God is releasing from those "big sleeves." As J. Edwin Orr often preached, "Whenever God is about to do something new with His people, He always sets them to praying."

If this is true (and I find myself in full agreement), then we should not be surprised by the dramatic increase in signs and wonders being reported by missiologists and Christian leaders worldwide, or by the rapidly expanding global harvest of lost souls. These are signs offering us hope that the fulfillment of the Great Commission may be closer than we think.

Some Christian leaders believe there is ample biblical reason to anticipate even more occasions of the miraculous as we move toward the end of this present age and the completion of the Great Commission. The supernatural, they suggest, may become the norm rather than a seldom-seen phenomenon.

The word *supernatural* comes from the two words *super* and *natural*. *Super* means "above" or "greater than." *Natural* means "what is normal or common." Thus, an event or occurrence might be considered supernatural if it is above or greater than what is normal or common. *Miracle*, an overused word in today's culture, refers to "an event or action that apparently contradicts known scientific laws." A miracle might also be defined simply as "a remarkable thing" or "a marvel."

Events like the voice in the night heard by the young Muslim Abdulai are remarkable occurrences that appear to contradict known scientific laws. But should we classify them as biblical miracles?

Biblical Reasons for Signs and Wonders

Miraculous occurrences can be theologically controversial. But I am sure all believers agree that, when it comes to the miraculous, God can do whatever He wants.

Still, it is a matter of biblical record that signs and wonders accompanied many of the evangelistic advances of the early Church. The writer of the epistle to the Hebrews explained, for example, that signs and wonders confirmed the truth of our salvation:

> This salvation, which was first announced by the Lord, was confirmed to us by those who heard him. God also testified to it by signs, wonders and various miracles, and gifts of the Holy Spirit distributed according to his will.
>
> Hebrews 2:3–4

The apostle Paul emphasized the role of miracles in his own missionary work, confirming the reality of the Gospel:

> Therefore I glory in Christ Jesus in my service to God. I will not venture to speak of anything except what Christ has ac-

complished through me in leading the Gentiles to obey God by what I have said and done—by the power of signs and miracles, through the power of the Spirit.

Romans 15:17–19

Let's note what the Scriptures themselves reveal about miracles and why God performs them. It will help us measure the validity of signs and wonders today, especially as they relate to the acceleration of the worldwide harvest of people coming to Christ.

Miracles Reveal God

First, it is clear from a careful study of Scripture that God performs miracles to reveal His glory and that "the earth will be filled with the knowledge of the glory of the LORD" (Habakkuk 2:14).

An example of a miracle revealing God's glory is found early in the book of Joshua when two Israelites were sent to spy out the city of Jericho. They lodged in the house of the prostitute Rahab, but the king of Jericho heard about the intruders and demanded she produce them. Instead, Rahab hid them in stalks of flax on the roof and told the king's messengers the spies had fled. Then she told the Israelites,

> "I know that the LORD has given this land to you and that a great fear of you has fallen on us, so that all who live in this country are melting in fear because of you. We have heard how the LORD dried up the water of the Red Sea for you when you came out of Egypt, and what you did to Sihon and Og, the two kings of the Amorites east of the Jordan, whom you completely destroyed."

Joshua 2:9–10

Rahab's conclusion contains a key insight into the reason God performs miracles:

> "When we heard of it, our hearts melted and everyone's courage failed because of you, for the LORD your God is God in heaven above and on the earth below."

verse 11

Clearly God used these miracles to reveal His power and glory to those who might stand in the way of His ultimate plan.

Biblically speaking, then, we might consider putting all supposed signs and wonders to this test: Do they reveal something of the nature and character of God and His ways? And in the end, is God glorified through them by revealing Himself to those who do not know Him?

Miracles Reveal Christ

A second reason for the miraculous is to reveal and glorify Jesus Christ. The apostle John, like the other gospel writers, described many miracles that Jesus performed. Then, after recounting the resurrection and how Jesus confronted the doubts of Thomas, John concluded:

> Jesus did many other miraculous signs in the presence of his disciples, which are not recorded in this book. But these are written that you may believe that Jesus is the Christ, the Son of God, and that by believing you may have life in his name.

John 20:30–31

The miracles Jesus performed, then, attested to the truth of who He was (and is!). And since we know that "Jesus Christ is the same yesterday and today and forever" (Hebrews 13:8), we should not be surprised to see miracles continue in ways that reveal and glorify Jesus, especially in convincing the lost of His reality.

Thus, we can put signs and wonders to this second test: Do they reveal the Person and work of our Lord Jesus Christ as the only way to salvation? Do they truly bring glory to Jesus?

Miracles Reveal God's Mercy

A third biblical purpose for miracles is to reveal the mercy of God and His unfathomable forgiveness and compassion, especially for those lost in sin. For reasons beyond our ability to explain or understand, God sometimes performs miracles simply out of His mercy. Feeding the five thousand (see John 6), feeding the four thousand (see Mark 8) and raising the widow's son from the dead in Elisha's day (see 2 Kings 4) are examples.

James, the brother of our Lord, referred to those who endured pain and suffering until victory came:

> Brothers, as an example of patience in the face of suffering, take the prophets who spoke in the name of the Lord. As you know, we consider blessed those who have persevered. You have heard of Job's perseverance and have seen what the Lord finally brought about. The Lord is full of compassion and mercy.
>
> James 5:10–11

Job was blessed after he suffered simply because God chose to manifest His mercy and compassion on him. We cannot discount that God, in His sovereignty, may choose to perform the supernatural in certain situations purely because He wants to.

And wasn't the redemption of lost people often key to these manifestations of the miraculous in Scripture? Consider Saul of Tarsus. He did not deserve the supernatural Damascus road encounter that resulted in his conversion (compare Acts 7:60 and 8:1 with Acts 9:1–9) any more than Abdulai Masa in North Africa deserved to hear a voice in the night.

God simply chose to save Paul in that way to reveal His mercy and compassion, prompting a third and final biblical test we might use to measure the validity of ostensible signs and wonders: Is there a strong basis to believe that God has acted sovereignly in this situation to manifest His mercy? Does the miracle measure up to a biblical understanding of God's way of showing His compassion so that people might know Him?

Theological disputes aside—specifically regarding the issue of whether miracles ceased with the apostles or continue to the present day—we must ask if there is any reason the miraculous would *not* have the same effect today as in early Church times. That is, wouldn't miracles today have the same impact in confirming the reality of the Gospel and drawing more people to a saving knowledge of Jesus Christ?

Dreams and Visions

The late Dr. Bill Bright, founder of Campus Crusade for Christ and one of my personal mentors, reported in an August 1995 letter to Campus Crusade partners the "astounding phenomenon" of dreams and visions confirming the reality of Christ, particularly among Muslims.

Thousands of letters from Muslims in North Africa and the Middle East, responding to a radio program aired throughout the region, describe dreams in which Jesus appeared to them, saying, "I am the way." When these Muslims heard the radio broadcast, they understood what they had experienced in their dreams and requested more information about this person called Jesus.

Dr. Bright also reported numerous Muslims in Algeria who had dreamed about Jesus. Later they discovered that their friends had had the very same dream, right down to the words Jesus had spoken. Several of these Muslims obtained Bibles and formed a small Bible study group, which grew rapidly.

One fanatical Muslim woman, who was nearing the conclusion of a four-year prison term for political activities, had a vision of Jesus in her cell. Jesus explained to her personally the meaning of redemption, she testified, so she surrendered her life to Him. Today she is ministering to Muslims as a staff worker with Campus Crusade for Christ.

These wonders are by no means confined to North Africa, nor was the voice in the night that confronted Abdulai Masa the only such encounter reported by Every Home for Christ workers. Thousands of miles away, in Kashmir in northeast India, a devout Muslim named Jalaluddin had a visitation just as remarkable.

Jalaluddin had studied the Koran faithfully for years. But as time passed, he felt increasingly dissatisfied with the Islamic message. No Christian worker had ever visited Jala, nor had he ever heard the Gospel, but Jala knew something was missing. Every attempt to find true peace eluded him.

One night while in a deep sleep, Jala had a dream. A man wearing a white robe appeared before him, asking, "Do you want real peace?"

"Yes," Jala replied. "I am seeking peace but I've been unable to find it."

"Read the holy Scripture."

"What is the holy Scripture and where can I get it?"

"The holy Scripture is the Holy Bible, and you can get it from the India Every Home Crusade, 3 Bishop Rockey Street, Faizabad Road, in Lucknow."

So vivid was the message that Jala sat straight up in bed. The address was etched in his mind. He grabbed a piece of paper and wrote it down.

A few days later the EHC office in Lucknow received Jala's letter, which said, in part:

> I don't know who you people are or whether this address is correct, but I am writing exactly as I was told in a dream. If you receive this, would you please immediately send me something that is called a "Holy Bible"?

About ten days later, Jala received the first lesson of a Bible correspondence course, along with the Bible he had requested. Soon he had completed all four lessons and read through the entire New Testament. Jala wrote once again to the EHC office, affirming two truths that Muslims often have great difficulty accepting: "The course has enlightened me about the reality of the Trinity, as well as the truth of the Sonship of Jesus Christ."

Within weeks Jala was attending a Christian church and witnessing freely to other Muslims about his newfound faith in Christ.

Kashinath's Confirmation

Hindus are also being touched by the supernatural—like Kashinath Hayak of the remote village of Pandiapathar, India. Located in the state of Orissa, in a dense forest about 140 miles from Orissa's capital city of Bhubaneswar, Pandiapathar is a Hindu village filled with anti-Christian sentiment.

Kashinath grew up in a hut made from thatched leaves and mud. His ancestors were strict Hindus, worshiping many deities, idols and demon spirits. He could not recall a true sense of peace or meaning from his early years. The people of his village had always quarreled. As far as Kashinath was concerned, no one knew true happiness.

And always they had to honor their gods. Religious festivals were all-consuming, and there were so many of them. Orissa Hindus liked to say, "There are thirteen festivals in twelve months," and a good Hindu was expected to take part in each of them.

One sweltering, humid morning, an EHC worker named Saral Singh from Bhubaneswar came to Pandiapathar—one of many villages in the district that workers like Saral had been assigned to reach with the Gospel. Soon he stood at the entry of Kashinath's modest thatched hut. Saral explained that only through Jesus Christ could one find eternal salvation. And it was really very simple, he added. No painful rituals were involved. There was a simple gift called "grace" that made it all possible. Forgiveness was free, final and forever. All Kashinath had to do was believe.

But believing seemed impossible for the well-trained Hindu. All his life Kashinath had been taught that it was necessary to honor many rituals and customs in order to satisfy his deity. Hinduism as a religion just made more sense. Surely, he reasoned, salvation had to be earned by worshiping many gods, and required far more than the simple faith this evangelist described.

So Kashinath rejected the message of Saral Singh.

But early the next morning, just before waking, Kashinath had a dream in which he saw a man standing before him dressed in beautiful white clothing.

"Kashinath," asked the Man, "how many parents do you have?"

"One father and one mother."

"Why, then, do you worship so many gods and goddesses? I am Jesus, the true way to God the Father."

With that Kashinath awoke from his deep sleep. It was early morning, and he set out immediately to find the evangelist.

Brother Saral Singh had not yet left the village, and he listened intently as Kashinath described his unusual dream. Then the evangelist explained again the message of the Good News.

This time, when he spoke about Jesus, Kashinath knew exactly whom Saral was referring to. He had seen Him in his dream. And before mid-morning Kashinath had placed his trust in Christ.

Why? Because his life-changing dream had confirmed to him the reality of the Gospel.

So we should not be surprised if the spread of the Gospel continues to accelerate amid ever-increasing signs and wonders. Just look what God is doing! Everywhere a person gazes, he or she will see supernatural harvest wonders, as the accounts on the pages to come will attest. God has something wonderful up His sleeves. And remember, God has really big sleeves.

2
Mountains of Mystery

Rain fell in sheets for more than two hours as five chiefs from several nearby Kwaio villages sat on the dirt floor of the primitive thatched hut. In the adjacent hut, their beloved chief was dying. Because Haribo was so revered, and because there was no official system for appointing a successor to someone who had become a legend, they were meeting to determine what to do if he passed away.

Meanwhile, the old chief in the next hut lay in an "earth bed" carved out of the ground, where a few family members and friends attended him as he struggled for each breath.

Chief Haribo was the personification of a people to whom missiologists refer as "the unreached." The Gospel of Jesus Christ had reached the coastal areas of the island of Malaita in the Solomon Island chain in the 1880s, about the time Haribo was born. But the Good News had touched neither his village nor his area, though it was little more than ten miles as the crow flies from the coastal settlements that were home to several thriving churches. It was as if a veil had been held over the interior of Malaita.

It was not that no one had cared for the Kwaio people in this rugged mountain area. Attempts had been made early in the century to take the Gospel to the mountain Kwaios. But they were intensely fearful of outsiders and became known as a fierce people who rejected every attempt to reach them.

Some traced this fear back to 1927, not long after the first missionaries from Australia and New Zealand brought the Gospel to the people living along Malaita's coast. In that year William Bell, a district officer of Great Britain, which controlled the southern Solomon Islands at the time, came with a band of thirteen officials to survey the land for the purpose of taxing the people. But the mountain Kwaios, afraid the stranger and his small army had offended the gods of their territory, massacred the entire party at a settlement called Kwaiawbe. The British government in Australia responded by sending a warship to shell that part of Malaita in an attempt to let these "heathens" know who was boss. Before it was over, two hundred Kwaio people had been killed, creating an even greater animosity among them toward outsiders.

Over the years several missionaries attempting to Christianize the Kwaios in the interior met with a similar fate. Several Roman Catholic priests were martyred by the Kwaios as they tried to establish a base for the Catholic Church in the mountain region of the island. In 1965 a missionary from New Zealand was killed trying to evangelize the Kwaios. More recently, in 1975, the Kwaios killed a Seventh-Day Adventist medical missionary and his son. Some say it involved a dispute over land rather than the preaching of the Gospel. But it gave the impression once again to outsiders, Christian workers in particular, that the Kwaios were bent on resisting any incursion into their territory. Anyone who had attempted to preach to them—few in number and for the most part long before the Second World War—gave up quickly because there was no fruit.

All this is why Haribo had lived through more than one hundred annual yam harvests without ever hearing anything of the Gospel.

The Decision to Advance

In the spring of 1990, a team of Christian workers mobilized by Every Home for Christ underwent weeks of training for a systematic campaign to share the Gospel with the Kwaios right where they lived. Leading the team were two EHC workers from Fiji who had been part of an earlier campaign to reach that island chain in the southwest Pacific. All 106 of Fiji's inhabited islands had been visited by Christian workers, village by village and home by home, resulting in more than 35,000 new converts and seven hundred small groups of new believers.

Afterward, these two Fijian evangelists had responded to the challenge to branch out to other remote places throughout the estimated 23,000 inhabited islands in the Pacific, so that all unreached peoples could hear about Jesus. Specifically, Matthew and Sova had traveled a thousand miles northwest to the Solomon Islands, where many young workers were being trained to take the Good News of Jesus to all one hundred inhabited islands in the chain, dwelling by dwelling and hut by hut. Several thousand people had given their hearts to Jesus so far. And now the work had reached Malaita, the second-largest of the Solomon Islands after Guadalcanal.

The trained team of about thirty workers started where it was easiest to work, in the coastal area, where they visited every village and home. Now their work along the coast was concluding.

Sitting around the fire of their base camp in early May 1990, the evangelistic team—the older Fijian workers and the younger trainees—were discussing what to do next. One of the Fijians pointed to the rugged, hilly terrain of the interior of Kwaio.

"Are there people living there who have yet to hear about Jesus?" he asked.

"Yes," responded one of his younger colleagues. "It's one of the most difficult areas in all of the islands to evangelize because of the rugged terrain and the hostile people."

"Good," responded one of the Fijian workers, adding a faith-filled declaration: "Tomorrow we advance into the interior."

Someone raised a fervent objection, emphasizing the fierceness of the mountain Kwaios and their many taboos that would endanger outsiders. Another worker explained that anyone who had ever tried to penetrate the mountainous interior had been attacked by the Kwaios and either driven out or killed (probably an exaggeration). Another mentioned the Catholic priests and the Seventh-Day Adventist doctor and his son who had been murdered. Someone mentioned the story of the shelling of the Kwaios by the navy ship from Australia early in the century. It almost seemed as if a case were being built to suggest that the mountain Kwaios should be evangelized by some other group, if at all.

"Besides," as one worker stated, "someone tried to reach these people earlier this century and they wouldn't listen."

The discussion continued for some time. Then one of the Fijian brothers reminded the group that Christ's Great Commission included "all the world" and "every creature" (Mark 16:15, KJV), and that they had not come all the way from Fiji to leave the task unfinished.

Soon the influence of the older Fijians on the young trainees gained a foothold, and everyone agreed it was time to step out by faith and penetrate all the regions of East Kwaio. Still, concern was voiced all around the campfire. Many dangers existed in the interior. The people there lived much as they did centuries ago. Cannibalism had been practiced in the region as recently as the end of the last century. Who could know for sure if it had ceased? Also, the area was known to be controlled by demonic powers.

The workers finally agreed that before a team went into the East Kwaio mountains, they would spend at least seven days in fasting and prayer.

Prayer Preparation

The season of prayer began the following day. The evangelistic team used insights that came in prayer, as well as information from coastal Kwaios who had once lived in the interior, to list the demonic powers that controlled the region. Some of these Kwaios had become Christians and knew much about the powerful spiritual forces at work in the interior. Several were former witch doctors who could actually name the spirits worshiped by the Kwaios.

Soon the team had a list of at least 87 different evil spirits. Then, point by point, they confronted each spiritual force boldly in prayer. For seven days, each of the strongholds was assaulted by intensive, focused warfare prayer.

On the eighth day, twelve members of the team of thirty were selected to make the first trip into the mountains. This group was further divided into two-man teams, each of which would head in different directions into East Kwaio.

Kwaio Christians from the coast, especially the former witch doctors, taught the teams about taboos in the region. They explained, for example, that the people of the interior were intensely superstitious and fearful of the "gods" of other people. They did not want any "outside spirits" offending their gods. They also taught the young workers that once inside a village of mountain Kwaios, they must not pray in any noticeable way inside their huts, because the Kwaios believed this would offend their gods.

Two of the young workers, Jack Alfred and Japta Labo, both relatively young Christians, were about to face this taboo firsthand. Thankfully, they (like the other members of the team) were operating under unusual divine protection and spiritual authority resulting from the seven days of fasting and prayer. (Some of the team would continue their fast for thirty days.) Unbeknownst to the believers, Kwaio priests in the interior would be able to sense this protection and authority.

On the eighth day, Jack and Japta joined ten other Christian workers, including Matthew and Sova, on the daylong trek into the remote hill country. The journey took them over some of the most jagged rocks imaginable. Once they reached the outer edges of the interior, the twelve workers split into two-man teams, so each could move through the region and visit every village they could find, keeping a record as they went of where the villages were located. No maps were available for the area, so teams would move as they sensed God leading them. Sometimes villages would seem to pop up out of nowhere, usually consisting of six to ten dwellings each. And often the way to determine where the next village lay hidden was to ask someone in the last village if another village was located nearby.

Jack and Japta headed off into the hills without an inkling they had a divine appointment. They were about to experience a miracle that would advance Christ's Kingdom dramatically among the Kwaios and prove to the evangelists that miracles still happen today.

A Divine Appointment

About five o'clock that afternoon, having picked their way all day over razor-sharp rocks, the two young Solomon Island workers stumbled onto a village. A warm mountain mist covered the hillside like a foggy shroud. A large gathering of people had assembled for some reason—considerably more people than the small population of the village. What was going on?

Jack and Japta were surrounded immediately by several large warriors, larger than most of the small-framed Kwaios. They wanted to know who these visitors were and why they had come. Jack explained as quickly as he could in the Kwaio language that they were bringing the Kwaio people Good News. But the burly guardians led them away to be questioned by five village priests or elders of the area. These were elders who had gathered in anticipation of the impending death of their chief. The strangers had arrived at a sacred moment and might be infringing on the customs of the Kwaios—a taboo of taboos that could meet with dire consequences.

As the area elders began to question the two EHC workers, many of the partially attired Kwaios standing about them held 24-inch machetes. Others gripped bows with poison-tipped arrows. Jack and Japta could not help recalling the rumors about the fierceness of the Kwaios. The ensuing conversation was tense.

The elders asked the workers why they were there.

"We have come to share Good News," the workers explained again, describing the one true God who had created everything—the hills, the trees, the animals, even the Kwaio people themselves.

"Our eternal God," they said, "sent His only Son to be like us, a Man, and to sacrifice His own life willingly on our behalf."

The visiting elders had never heard a message like this and discussed among themselves whether it could possibly be true. Some thought it might be. The others thought it was impossible. They did understand the concept of a blood sacrifice because they had done this often with arrivals.

Then a spokesman told the evangelists, "We cannot believe anything you say unless our chief believes."

The workers had been trained to adapt to other cultures when sharing the Gospel. They knew it was customary to get permission from the chief of a village or area before doing anything, and that, once they had such permission, they could go everywhere freely since their presence had been blessed by the chief. So Jack and Japta requested permission to see the chief.

The elders refused. Their respected chief was very old and dying, they said, and seeing him was out of the question.

Then one of the workers had an idea.

"When Jesus Christ came as the Son of God," he explained to the elders, "He came not only to deliver men from their sins, but to heal sick people, too. God is quite capable of healing your chief."

Two of the five attending elders felt the workers should be given a chance to talk with the chief. Two others disagreed. One was uncertain. So about seven in the evening, two hours after they had arrived at the village, the young workers were placed in seclusion in a nearby hut while the elders engaged in a prolonged discussion.

The two elders who agreed with the young men suggested they be given a chance to pray to their God for the chief's healing. The two in opposition were certain this would offend their gods and cause them to seek retribution. Finally the elder who had not made up his mind became convinced these young men might represent a God who had great power and just possibly might restore Chief Haribo—no matter how many yam harvests he had lived—to see yet another.

Jack and Japta waited the entire night locked in the hut. Careful not to appear to be praying, they could see and hear through the thatched walls as the elders argued incessantly around a fire. The elders appeared to be chewing a special nut from a particular tree in East Kwaio that Jack and Japta had heard about. It had a druglike effect, keeping them awake and making them unusually talkative.

At seven in the morning the elders finally returned. The two workers would be permitted to pray for the chief.

A Being in White

Jack and Japta could see, as soon as they entered the hut of Haribo, how very sick the old chief was as he lay in his earth bed, struggling for breath. If they had understood his condition, would they have been more careful in explaining their theology of healing to the elders? In any case, rather than speak to him about physical healing or even pray for his healing, Jack shared with him quickly God's plan of salvation, explaining that Jesus was the only way to eternal life.

Haribo was fascinated with the message.

"I have waited my entire lifetime to hear this story," he said. "I have always felt there was some sacred message like this. But no one ever came to bring us such words. How can I receive this Jesus into my life?"

Jack and Japta led Chief Haribo in a simple sinner's prayer. And a few moments later, God's peace seemed to fill Haribo's eyes. It was clear, even to the village elders, that something remarkable had occurred. So they permitted the two young workers to leave.

About two hours later the old chief died. The attending elders sent a villager running after the workers to bring them back. Perhaps they blamed them for offending their gods and thereby killing their chief with their prayers. Possibly they wanted the workers to pray once again that their chief would be restored. But the villager did not find the workers and returned alone.

Chief Haribo lay in his earth bed the entire day, lifeless now, as his body was prepared for the traditional Kwaio burial. The elders waited just outside his hut. Then, about five in the afternoon, Haribo sat up quietly and began to speak.

"Let the elders gather," he said, to the utter amazement of those standing nearby. "And let someone go and find the boys who came earlier to tell me about Jesus."

No one had seen anything like it. Their beloved chief, who had lain lifeless all day, had come back from the dead. Now Haribo, who had captivated villagers for many yam harvests with his stories, told a remarkable account.

A being dressed in glorious white (apparently the Kwaios have no word in their language for *angel*) had taken him a great distance to the most beautiful place he had ever seen. There a person called Jesus Christ, the Son of God the young men had told him about, was being worshiped by a huge crowd of people. The glorious being explained to him that this beautiful place was where people who believed in Jesus would go for all eternity to worship Him. So everything the boys had said was true.

Peace had come to his life, Haribo said, and he had no more pain, nor had he seen any suffering among the people who worshiped Jesus. Haribo also spoke of meeting several important people to whom this being in white introduced him. He gave the names of various Old Testament prophets.

Then the being in white showed him another place—a place of great torment where people go who reject the message of

Jesus that these boys had brought to the mountains. Finally the being in white explained that it was necessary for Haribo to go back to the Kwaio people for a short time to tell the elders of his village that the message was true. They needed to listen to what the young men from the coast were saying about this person called Jesus. This Jesus was their only way to experience eternal life.

Finally the old chief commissioned runners to find the workers from the coast and bring them back to preach to the people.

This time Jack and Japta were found and brought back. Astounded at what had happened to the old chief, they presented the message of salvation again, this time to the entire village. Every person, including Chief Haribo's immediate family of 21 members, received Christ as their Savior. And soon more than three hundred villagers throughout the area (consisting of ten nearby villages) had surrendered their lives to Christ.

Haribo remained alive all that night and into the next morning. Then he lay back down quietly in his earth bed and went to be forever with Jesus.

The Healing Stone

In April 1995 I traveled to the island of Malaita and took a helicopter journey into the rugged interior region of East Kwaio. There I talked with one of the workers who witnessed the events that took place in Haribo's village in May 1990.

Not long after, six full-time EHC missionaries from Fiji went to live among the Kwaios in Malaita's interior. But the village in which Haribo lived and died has disappeared. After the evangelization of East Kwaio, in 1993 the new converts burned their huts as an act of repentance and moved to

Bobota, a larger Christian community near the coast. It is not uncommon, I learned, for new believers to set fire to their huts and all their possessions as a symbol of forsaking the past and separating themselves from the demonic powers they believe once occupied their dwellings.

This helps to explain why Christian workers who enter a Kwaio village are not allowed to pray, especially in a villager's hut. One superstitious Kwaio woman told an EHC worker, "We know that your God is stronger than our god. And if you pray in our home, your God may have a victory in that moment, but when you leave, your God will go with you, and our god will stay here and beat us up."

Today as many as eight thousand Kwaios have come to know Jesus Christ, including well over a thousand in the most remote areas of the island where our helicopter landed. I saw firsthand the way unconverted villagers seem to come out of nowhere, fascinated to hear the Gospel.

I was also amazed that our helicopter trip from the capital city of Honiara on Guadalcanal Island into the interior of Kwaio took little more than an hour. And from the place our helicopter landed on the coast of Malaita, where coastal Kwaios first heard the Gospel a century ago, it is only a seven-minute helicopter flight into the remote areas where many had never heard about Jesus even once. Unchecked satanic bondage must have held this area in darkness for generations.

One subsequent dramatic event in 1992, two years after Haribo died, proved another supernatural breakthrough for the interior Kwaio people. Like the miracle at Haribo's village, this was the result of a sustained call to fasting and prayer. And it affirms a premise made by missions strategist Ed Silvoso: "It always takes a power encounter of some sort to establish the Church for the first time, because the Church has to displace the existing satanic structure."[1]

This power encounter concerned a prayer confrontation with a Kwaio stronghold called "the healing stone." The stone was a large boulder in a village called Cinaragu, located deep in East Kwaio in an area especially revered by the Kwaios. The stone, easily the size of one of the two-man tents we stayed in during our visit to Kwaio territory, represented a key site for pagan worship in the area. It was there that the people of the hills had offered sacrifices to their gods, perhaps for generations.

Christian workers who had been in East Kwaio for only a matter of months soon learned that the healing stone and its immediate surroundings were off-limits to outsiders. Even walking on the ground close to the giant stone could endanger their lives. The healing stone, they recognized, was a stronghold of Satan representing obvious control over the region. It was a "power point" (a symbol or place that seems to be a focal point for demonic activity) more significant than a mere taboo held by the locals.

So another week of fasting and prayer was scheduled, this one specifically targeting the huge stone. For seven days several Christian workers stood on a mountainside opposite the healing stone—their "prayer mountain," as the evangelists called it—praying against this pagan object of worship.

On a cloudy day, as the warriors concluded their seven days of prayer and fasting, a Kwaio priest made his way to the stone to offer a sacrifice. At that moment a bolt of lightning darted from the cloudy sky and struck the stone, splitting it in two. Half of the huge stone rolled down the steep mountain. The priest turned and ran, dropping his sacrifice in the confusion.

Several village priests of the region testified later that when they heard lightning had hit the rock, they were overcome with fear. And a few days later, one of the chiefs of the area near the stone invited the evangelists to come and preach about their Jesus.

Not only did all those present invite Christ into their hearts, but the priests asked the evangelists if the villagers could move with their families to Bobota, the new village peopled by Kwaio converts. The evangelists agreed, and these new converts from several villages promptly burned their huts, too, as an act of repentance, and moved to Bobota.

The breaking of the huge healing stone by a divine lightning bolt was one more outward sign that a powerful stronghold of Satan had been broken over the interior region of East Kwaio.

Mountains of Majesty

During our visit to the new Christian village of Bobota, I was given the privilege of cutting a special red ribbon brought up from the coast that adorned the entrance of the area's first-ever primary school. Seven non-Christian chiefs, who had pleaded for their children to attend the school and learn to read, came from neighboring villages to watch our ribbon-cutting ceremony.

Later I learned that of the first 25 students enrolled in the school, fourteen were children from unconverted villages. And not long afterward, the chiefs from those villages came to the pastor in Bobota and announced that they, too, wanted to become followers of Jesus. One of the chiefs, who had moved with his family to the village just before we arrived, was an old head chief for the Kafu tribe—a smaller tribe from within East Kwaio.

The Kafu people, I learned, are much like the Pygmies of Africa. They do little if any planting and harvesting, living off the land instead. But the Kafu people, unlike the Pygmies, subsist primarily by stealing whatever they can. They also have been known to kill, if necessary, to survive.

Now the old chief, Sumete, stood before me smiling brightly, though most of his teeth had been eaten away by decay. Through an interpreter, he told me his story. He had been the priestly chief of the entire Kafu people, a small tribe of at most three thousand people. As Kafu high priest as well as tribal chief, Sumete had stolen three hundred pigs in his lifetime and sacrificed an additional five hundred pigs to their "devils" on behalf of other Kafu people. He had kept count!

About two months before, Sumete had become deathly ill and, seeking a cure, had offered thirty pigs, an amazing number for a Kafu, to an evil spirit. But his condition only worsened. Then the devil told him he must go kill somebody. For the first time, a strange new voice within Sumete told him this would be wrong. (This happened soon after the healing stone was destroyed by lightning, just a short distance from where Sumete lived.)

Never had he received such an impression. And when the Kafu chief heard what was happening in the Christian village, he decided to visit. There he surrendered his life to Christ and, a few days later, changed his name to Peter, after that of the apostle.

When I met Peter in April 1995, he and his family had just burned their hut and all their possessions, even though they had no place to live until a new hut was built in Bobota. And this would take several weeks, because huge stalks from a special kind of palm tree near the coast had to be transported by foot up the jagged mountains to make the thatched roofs for huts in Kwaio villages, and each trip to bring a single armload of the unique palm fronds required eight to ten hours. So, until their new hut was finished, Peter and his family were sleeping under the trees, trying to avoid the often-torrential rains.

My heart was touched, especially knowing that joining Peter and his family are hundreds of Kwaios and Kafu alike, scattered throughout the remote regions of Malaita, who have met Jesus as Savior. They are the fruit of a small army of courageous young believers who trekked tirelessly throughout the rugged interior of East Kwaio. Their sacrifices have helped transform those once-feared mountains of mystery into glorious, Christ-honoring mountains of majesty.

3
People of the Trees

It would take eleven days traveling by canoe up the mighty Zaire River (also known as the Congo) before the two Every Home for Christ pioneer missionaries from Kinshasa would reach their destination deep in the equatorial rainforest. From the Zaire River they would journey several days more against the strong current up the smaller Momboyo River. From the Momboyo they would journey still deeper into the forest on small tributaries, until they reached the heart of the rainforest rarely seen by outsiders. It was a dangerous journey few ever made.

The farther these missionaries plunged into the forest, the more difficult their task became. The larger motorized canoes available for hire along the enormous Zaire River could not be used on the smaller tributaries.

Deep in the forest, the missionaries enlisted Pygmy guides to take them even farther into the jungle. Sometimes along the tiny tributaries they all had to get out of their canoes and push them through the thick vegetation. Once back in their small vessels, they quickly pulled bloodsucking leeches off one another's bodies.

The guides knew where their fellow nomadic people lived. They were hidden in the trees.

On their journey, the workers would visit a tribe of six thousand Pygmies. Their young chief, Lendongo, just like the old priest Haribo of the Kwaio people, would be one of the first of the tribe to profess Jesus as Savior. Then multitudes would follow, and two rainforests on opposite sides of the world would shine brightly in the light of God's Son.

What I could never have imagined is that I was soon to see with my own eyes the fruit of the labor of these EHC pioneer missionaries. At least four thousand of the six thousand Pygmies in the area would profess Christ in less than 24 months. And especially amazing: I would see handwritten lists of all their names! But first I had to travel to "the end of the world."

The Most Dangerous Place on Earth

It is, quite simply, the world's most horrible way to die. The virus is called Ebola Zaire because it was first traced in 1967 to an outbreak along the Ebola River in northern Zaire, an area containing some of the deadliest diseases known to man. The 1967 outbreak occurred at the Yambuku Mission Hospital run by Belgian nuns and killed almost all of the nurses, followed by the nuns, in a matter of days. Soon the disease erupted (seemingly simultaneously) in 55 villages surrounding the hospital.

I would have known little of the disease or its origin had it not been for the intensity with which the woman at the visa service office pleaded with us not to go to Zaire (now known as the Democratic Republic of Congo).

A ministry colleague and I had planned for some time to travel deep into the rainforest of Central Africa. We wanted to see firsthand the amazing results being reported among remote Pygmy tribes coming to Jesus. The numbers of new converts in such a short time, as well as churches planted among these indigenous peoples, were so remarkable as to seem beyond imagination.

If the reports were true—and we needed to confirm them ourselves—a powerful model was emerging that we believed could help touch scores, if not hundreds, of similar unreached peoples globally.

But first we had to get to Zaire, and a woman at our local visa service considered it her obligation to warn us of the dangers.

"The State Department has issued a travel advisory for the region because of the instability of the government," she said. "It's probably the most dangerous place on earth you could visit right now. And I'm sure you're aware they have the worst diseases in the world."

Neither the woman nor I knew the Ebola virus was just resurfacing in the heart of Zaire, not too far south of where we were heading in the coming week. And just north of our destination of the Momboyo River was the Ebola River, where the disease had first appeared a little more than two decades earlier. We were headed right for the middle of it all.

For one of the few times in my extensive travels, I inwardly questioned going on a trip. Little did I realize that the enemy did not want us to see the fruit of what can happen in so remote a region if believers will simply go there with the Gospel.

Heading for a Hot Zone

The same weekend that I talked with the woman in the visa office, a popular motion picture titled *Outbreak* was released, based on the ravages of the Ebola Zaire virus. The film begins with a scene depicting the heart of Zaire's rainforest, precisely where we were heading.

A few days later Richard Preston, author of the *New York Times* bestseller *The Hot Zone*, appeared on "The 700 Club" with Pat Robertson to discuss not only the seriousness of diseases like the Ebola virus, but the fact that similar, if not more deadly, diseases might be lurking in other regions of the world like Zaire's rainforests. (The AIDS virus is thought to have originated in the same region of northern Zaire.) The term *hot zone* used by Preston is a medical description given to any area of the world in which a deadly virus such as Ebola is currently active and transmittable.[1]

A friend who knew of our plans to go to Zaire that week and who watched "The 700 Club" called with a strange feeling she had had during prayer. She wanted to warn me not to go.

Having read Richard Preston's description of the Ebola virus, I could understand why. When the virus attacks a human body, every organ and tissue (except skeletal muscle and bone) is affected. Preston calls the virus the perfect parasite, because it transforms virtually every part of the body into something like a digested slime of virus particles that cannot wait to find their way into other hosts—meaning other human bodies. Once this happens, as the author explains, the virus simply "turns the body to mush, and the under layers of skin die and liquefy."

Next, spontaneous rips appear in the skin, and the blood begins to pour from the small rips. Red spots on the skin appear, grow and spread, and then combine to become huge, ugly bruises. The skin becomes so loose it almost falls off the body. Everything begins to bleed. The mouth begins to bleed, as well as the gums and nose. Blood oozes from even the ears and eyes. In fact, a person attacked by the Ebola virus will have eyeballs so filled with blood that they literally weep blood. Soon every opening in the body, no matter how small, bleeds. And all this happens in only a few days.

Finally the victim, whose brain has become clogged with dead blood cells, experiences *grand mal* epileptic convulsions. And as the whole body twitches and shakes, blood spreads everywhere, allowing the virus to spread easily to others who are unprotected.

Ebola is indeed a horrible disease, and anyone heading into the region where it all began should think twice before going. But what occupied my thoughts the most was how much the Ebola virus reminded me of the ultimate ravages of sin that so totally destroys its host—the human soul. Zaire, I knew, with its huge rainforests—along with every other region of the world controlled by Satan—is a spiritual hot zone, sending lost humanity to a fate far worse than any deadly earthly virus.

Jesus is the only cure, I was convinced, and I had to see with my own eyes how the Cure was coming to the rainforests of central Africa.

The Power of a Prayer Shield

Despite what I knew was the harassment of the enemy, my colleague and I soon found ourselves in Kinshasa, Zaire, loading our small tents and other supplies—including one hundred pounds of salt for the Pygmies—into a small Mission Aviation Fellowship plane. It would take us deep into the equatorial rainforest.

Central Africa, including the nation of Zaire, is host to many of the world's great rainforests. After South America, Africa holds more intact tropical forests than any continent on earth. And the largest share of these forests is in Zaire, followed by the Republic of Congo, which borders Zaire to the west.

Thankfully we had found a courageous MAF pilot willing to take us to a rugged landing strip at an encampment called Boteka, located along the Momboyo River. It would serve as the launching pad for our trip still deeper into the forest. Had we made the journey that the EHC workers had made two years earlier, it would have taken eleven days from Kinshasa by canoe up the mighty Zaire (Congo) River before we even reached the Momboyo. Then it would have taken several more days of canoe travel to bring us to Boteka. From there we would have faced an even longer journey to our final destination, the village of Bosuka, where hundreds of Pygmies were turning to Jesus. But, as it was, the MAF flight took us only three hours.

Beneath us, dense jungle seemed to stretch endlessly like a plush shag carpet of a hundred shades of green. The canopy of lush foliage was broken periodically by small lakes and what seemed to be countless snaking rivers. *How impossible it would be*, I thought, *to land a single-engine plane like this in such a dense jungle if there were an emergency.* As if to heighten my concern, we were flying straight into huge, billowing clouds with raindrops ripping against the windshield and lightning dancing just beyond our wingtips. Yet the plane flew steady as an arrow.

Having flown more than forty times around the world in every kind of weather condition, I was amazed how the Lord guided our MAF pilot straight through the weather with hardly a bump. Then, as we neared the Momboyo River, I looked down at the handmade booklet of several hundred names that I had been clutching in my hand for the last three hours. Did these names have something to do with the smooth flight?

Prepared by my secretary, Debbie Lord, it was a booklet of about twenty 8 ½ by 11 inch pages of single-spaced names of people praying for us every minute we were on this journey. It was part of a special prayer shield launched by Every Home for Christ. Each name appeared under the specific time that person would be praying. Not a moment of our entire journey, day or night, lacked at least a few people praying; and during the three hours we had been in the air, even though it was the middle of the night back home, more than forty intercessors had been praying continuously.

Because we had an extra seat in the small MAF plane, we had taken along with us a Belgian nun from Zaire who had close friends she had not seen in several years at the encampment at Boteka. She had been concerned about taking the rigorous, almost two-week journey by canoe and was excited about being able to travel with us by plane. So she had contacted the sisters of Boteka by ham radio to ask if we could use their large, forty-foot canoe, with not one but two outboard motors. Because we were providing free travel to their fellow nun, the sisters of Boteka were pleased to let us use their large canoe for continuing our journey even deeper into the forest once we had arrived in Boteka.

Already we were seeing how beautifully God was putting things together for our journey.

The Last Tree on Earth

The plane landed safely on a patch of grass in Boteka, which I soon learned had been a Belgian Catholic mission since the early 1950s. (Zaire was known then as the Belgian Congo.) I also discovered that the Every Home Crusade ministry had already seen significant results in the region around Boteka. In fact, many of the Pygmies and Bantu people (taller Africans) who stood cheering along the small grass landing strip when we arrived were converts of EHC's systematic every-home evangelism ministry in the Boteka area.

Teams of EHC workers from throughout the region also had come, some traveling by motorless canoes for days, traversing some of the many smaller rivers of the region. Our African leadership had had no contact with these evangelists for months, but we soon learned how plentiful the harvest of souls had been since the work began in this part of the forest not much more than 36 months earlier.

At daybreak the next day, just before 6 A.M., we climbed into our borrowed forty-foot canoe to begin what would be a fourteen-hour journey against the strong current of the snake-like Momboyo River. We would not arrive at our destination, an encampment called Imbonga, until eight o'clock that night. In the same time it would take to travel by canoe from Boteka to Imbonga, probably little more than 75 miles, a Boeing 747 could take us from San Francisco to Hong Kong.

The Momboyo was one of hundreds, if not thousands, of rivers that flow throughout the several rainforests of Central Africa. As I looked at a map, I noticed, not too far north, the name of another river I recognized—the Ebola. Being reminded of that name made me a little uneasy.

As we motored down the Momboyo River, it again seemed to me that the forest was a vast carpet of greenery, thirty to sixty feet high, reaching to the water's edge as if to drink incessantly. On our entire fourteen-hour journey, we never saw another motorized canoe. Frequently, however, we saw Bantu in their small one- or two-man canoes, darting in and out of tributaries that seemed to flow from everywhere into the river.

Finally we arrived at Imbonga, another Catholic encampment even more remote than Boteka, that would launch us still farther into the jungle. We faced an additional 32-kilometer (twenty-mile) trek by foot, or possibly bicycle, even deeper into the forest the following day.

The Catholics of Imbonga had the only vehicle within hundreds of kilometers—an old, beat-up Land Rover—but according to a report we had received by "canoe courier" earlier in the week, we would not be able to use the vehicle because numerous log bridges along the narrow jungle road had decayed and were no longer passable. So we were happy to discover upon our arrival that two EHC workers who had heard of our coming several weeks earlier had mobilized a small army of Bantu and Pygmies to repair the bridges.

Then we learned that the narrow road—not much more than a twelve-foot-wide jungle clearing stretching for 32 kilometers—included 222 separate log bridges, crossing over an equal number of small rivers and tiny streams. Each bridge consisted of little more than ten or twenty thick logs. Often our team of five had to get out of the aging Land Rover because the logs appeared too weak. But only once did any of the logs give way, and thankfully, with a hand-operated winch and a long chain that our Bantu guide attached to a huge tree, we were able to pull the Land Rover from the ravine and make it to our final destination.

Along the 32-kilometer journey from Imbonga to the Pygmy settlement of Bosuka, we saw numerous Bantu villages—not uncommon in the area. Pygmy villages, on the other hand, were highly unusual, since Pygmies tend to be nomadic, seldom settling down to live in conventional huts or dwellings.

It reminded me of when the Every Home Crusade began in the forest three years earlier. None of the initial progress reports from our workers had indicated how many homes were being reached, even though this statistic appears on every report coming to our central office from the field. Only as we know the precise number of homes being visited in a region can we measure the approximate number of people being reached daily with the Gospel. (The world average is 5.2 persons living in each home.) But our area director had been reporting only the numbers of conversions (and subsequent baptisms) among the Pygmies. So we asked him for updated reports that included the number of actual homes being reached.

Our director responded in writing that the Pygmies live in trees, not homes.

Remembering those old Tarzan movies that depicted natives living in tree houses, I wrote back that even a tree hut is a home, and asked our brother to report the number of tree houses reached.

He wrote again suggesting we still did not understand. The Pygmies do not live in homes, houses or even huts in the trees. They just live and sleep in the trees, sometimes on the thick leaves, sometimes under them and sometimes in temporary thatched shelters assembled hastily when a tribe moves to a new area for hunting. Occasionally they even tie themselves into a tree, he wrote, so they will not *fall* asleep (quite literally!) from a high tree and injure themselves.

This report from our director ended with usual African humor: "Brother Dick, we have now launched EHC's very first Every Tree Crusade." Then he modified our long-standing goal, which speaks of reaching "the last home on earth with the Gospel," by printing in large letters on his report: "WE WILL NOT STOP UNTIL WE REACH THE LAST TREE ON EARTH WITH THE GOSPEL!"

Now, as the well-worn Land Rover finally rolled into the village of Bosuka, I realized instantly we were in Pygmy territory. The broadened path now became a road filled with

Pygmy believers waving palm branches joyously and greeting us with Pygmy dances. They were singing a lively song, which I soon learned they had written themselves and which declared repeatedly, "Jesus is Lord and He's coming back again!"

The settlement called Bosuka meant "the end of the world" in their Pygmy dialect, for not much lies beyond Bosuka but dense forest. Indeed, the very village of Bosuka did not even exist until relatively recently. But here I was, standing among these usually nomadic "people of the trees" and seeing with my own eyes that they had formed a village with a church at its center. It was a Christian phenomenon, I was told, and had resulted in thousands of Pygmies in the area giving their lives to Christ.

Half an Arm's Length

The work had gone slowly at first. The two EHC workers who had come to this part of the forest fourteen months earlier—not for a visit but to live—were a married couple, both Bantu.

But as far back as anyone can remember, the smaller Pygmies have feared the larger Bantu. They learned to trade with them for precious commodities not available in the deep forest, commodities like salt and metal (the latter to make tools and weapons), but for generations the Bantu had slaughtered the Pygmies and driven them even deeper into the forest.

Pygmies are the world's shortest people. Because they are unable to process the hormones needed for normal growth, adults reach an average height of only four feet six inches.[2] Pygmies feel they are second-class human beings—like monkeys, perhaps, or a category of human just above the animals. Their very name derives from the Greek word *pygme*, which means "half an arm's length."

The Pygmy sense of inferiority made it difficult at first for the Bantu workers to make even an initial presentation of the Gospel. So they had to be unusually creative. They would go to a clearing, for example, where they knew Pygmies could see them, and leave a quantity of salt on an old tree stump or mound in the clearing. Then they would retreat into the shadows of the forest but stand near the edge so the Pygmies could see they were still there. Soon the Pygmies would come, ever so slowly, because they wanted the salt so desperately. Then they would snatch up the precious substance, leave monkey meat or fish in its place and rush off into the forest.

The Christians would come a third day, but this time they would wait only a few paces from the salt. Now it would take even more time for the Pygmies to cultivate the courage to come. But because salt is priceless to a Pygmy, a brave adult (usually a young warrior) would soon step into the clearing and move toward the salt. As he did, the Bantu Christians would walk very slowly toward the salt, trying to send a signal that they meant no harm.

Eventually at least one of the Pygmies, sometimes more, would muster enough courage to approach the believers waiting nearby with the salt. In this moment—through interpreters, if necessary—the Christian workers would begin to tell them they had come in a spirit of love with Good News for their people. The Pygmy listeners almost never looked into the eyes of the speaker, reflecting their conviction that they were less than human.

These first close encounters usually lasted only a few minutes, but they were crucial for building trust that might later lead to longer meetings. Still, in these first moments of contact, the Christians sought to share the Gospel message as quickly as possible. They never knew if they would get another opportunity.

Sometimes it took two or three encounters before there was an indication the message was being understood. When it was, it was clear something was happening in the heart of the recipient. The pattern was almost always the same. The Pygmy would agree to say the sinner's prayer, still not looking into the eyes of the believer. Then he or she would begin to weep, sometimes uncontrollably. Then, just as suddenly, as one worker described the process to me, "The Pygmy will lift his head boldly, look you straight in the eye and laugh with joy. We know then that something has really happened. The Pygmy has just met Jesus."

A Cornelius Conversion

When our team had finally arrived at Bosuka, we discovered that a groundswell of conversions had taken place over an amazingly short time. Our last report some six months earlier had indicated that as many as twelve hundred Pygmies in the Bosuka area had received Christ. But because of a lack of radio transmitters in this village, or any other communications from this deep in the forest, we did not know this number had grown significantly. There were now four thousand converts from a tribe of little more than six thousand. Two-thirds of the tribe had come to Jesus! (Two years later a report would indicate all six thousand had now professed Christ!)

One of these special converts—and one of the very first ones—was Lendongo Botshemba, the thirty-year-old chief of the tribe, who greeted us graciously on our arrival. His conversion, our director of the region told me, had been like that of Cornelius in Acts 10.

The young chief had grown up worshiping the snakes and trees of the dense rainforest along the Momboyo River, just as his parents Bokimba and Bolanza had before him. Most, if not all, of his tribe did not know they lived on a continent called Africa or in a nation now called the Democratic Republic of Congo. And neither Lendongo nor his parents had any idea that David Livingstone and other missionary pioneers had come to Africa more than 150 years earlier to bring the Good News of God's Son to their land.

But the miracle of the Gospel was now transforming these parts of the rainforest. Lendongo's entire family had been converted, affecting some forty persons in all. And churches were being planted to help nurture and sustain these new believers. Lendongo was responsible for the formation of at least eighteen additional Christian villages in the region, each one established around a church.

In a neighboring part of the equatorial rainforest, where we had heard that 32 churches had been planted by EHC workers 36 months earlier, we now learned that an astounding three hundred additional fellowships of new believers had been born. In still another rainforest area (in Cameroon, West Africa) five thousand more Pygmies were converted and baptized. Several hundred additional house churches were formed as a result.

The "Every Tree Crusade" launched in the rainforest had been responsible for more than fifteen thousand Pygmy conversions—*in just 36 months!* And as our journey to the people of the trees ended, and our large canoe headed back down the Momboyo River, I could not get a verse from Isaiah out of my mind: "The earth will be full of the knowledge of the Lord as the waters cover the sea" (Isaiah 11:9).

Look what God is doing—and rejoice!

4

Back in Fashion

Look, indeed, at what God is doing globally: there's no mistaking that the harvest is accelerating. In the year 2000, Every Home for Christ followed up with 756,000 new believers and those responding to EHC's home-to-home evangelism. In 2007 that number grew to more than 8,400,000 over a similar twelve-month period. Other ministries could report similar exponential advances. What's especially exciting about this last days' harvest is that it is remarkably simple and profoundly sweeping.

Early in my ministry, a wise colleague and mentor told me, "Dick, God's plans are always incredibly simple and unusually inexpensive. So if things start getting terribly complex and amazingly expensive, you might want to rethink whether it's God's plan after all."

The early Church must have understood this principle when it came to reaching the world for Jesus. All the believers had was a commission from Christ to go everywhere to everybody (see Mark 16:15) and a caution from Him to do it without monetary encumbrances or materialistic concerns (see Matthew 10:9–10).

As I explain in the pages that follow, those New Testament believers ultimately reached entire cities and regions with the Gospel of Jesus so that "everybody" heard (see Acts 4:16; 5:28; 13:44, 49; 19:10) without benefit of modern technology. Imagine—no laptops, BlackBerries, websites or iPods. Their method was unusually simple and amazingly economical. And I believe, as we will shortly see, that it is coming back into fashion.

Could It Be This Simple?

It was our very first missionary journey, and my wife, Dee, and I were excited. We were in our early twenties, serving as youth pastors of a growing church in southern Wisconsin while I finished my studies at Moody Bible Institute in Chicago. It was 1966. Our denomination had decided to begin a new program for young people, letting them experience missions firsthand on a short-term basis. We would have the joy of leading one of these very first teams of youth, just four in number, to a distant mission field. (Years later that number would grow to more than ten thousand.)

Our assignment was the Central American nation of British Honduras (now known as Belize). During our briefing sessions with veteran missionaries before the journey, including one long-term missionary from the country of our destination, we were informed that few mission fields in the world were more rugged than British Honduras. It was called the Africa of Central America. Indeed, when the veteran missionary from the region heard that a team of young people was going into British Honduras, he seriously questioned the wisdom of choosing such a location for so new a program, especially one that involved youth. We were told to expect the worst of conditions and not too many results.

Before we left on our journey, another veteran missionary suggested that distributing evangelistic literature might be the best thing we could do on our visit, since more and more Central Americans were learning to read. In fact, they had a passion for reading everything they could get their hands on. So we decided to spend most of our summer mission going home to home distributing literature.

As we walked from house to house in the shimmering heat of Belize City, the capital of British Honduras, we noticed people's hunger for the printed page. Not one person rejected the literature. Often those who were home wanted to hear more. We were amazed when more than 450 people in just five weeks invited us into their homes and prayed to receive Christ as Savior.

Late one night in the sweltering heat, I lay awake thinking about the simplicity of communicating the Gospel house to house and the unusual receptivity of the people. Why wasn't there a worldwide initiative to do just what we were doing? It seemed so logical, especially after 450 people had prayed to receive Christ in just over a month. At that time as many as three million people globally were becoming literate every week. *How relatively easy it would be to evangelize the vast majority of the world*, I thought, *if the global Church went systematically to where people lived, providing them a clearly printed message of salvation. If we could win the readers, they would surely witness to and win the nonreaders.*

And if this strategy were to be covered with much prayer, I further reasoned, I was sure the Holy Spirit would open the eyes of at least one reader in every home. And how simple it would be to include decision cards with the literature so people could send a response to a follow-up office and request Bible lessons to help them grow in their understanding of what it means to be a disciple of Jesus Christ.

As I lay awake in the night, the smoke of burning mosquito repellent filling the air, I wondered if world evangelism could really be this simple. Could Jesus have envisioned such a strategy when He gave His Great Commission to the early Church?

> "Go and make disciples of all nations, baptizing them in the name of the Father and of the Son and of the Holy Spirit, and teaching them to obey everything I have commanded you."
>
> Matthew 28:19–20 (see also Mark 16:15)

Little did I realize that night, as I pondered a home-to-home strategy for the fulfillment of the Great Commission, that God had already birthed just such a strategy. In fact, by this time it had been in place for more than thirteen years. Nor could I have known that in thirty years I would be involved in heading its international leadership, observing signs and wonders beyond imagination (as you will soon discover) that clearly indicate fulfilling the Great Commission could well be within reach of our generation.

A Biblical Pattern for Evangelizing the World

When Jesus discussed His ultimate return to earth and the establishment of His eternal Kingdom among humankind, He made it clear that one primary sign was central to the culmination of these events. The record of Christ's words to His disciples concerning this sign can be found in at least two key passages in the gospels. And both of these New Testament writers describe Him reaching the same *succinct =*

conclusion about the primary sign that must precede His return.

Mark records Jesus as describing a variety of events that would occur as indicators that the time of His return was approaching. Jesus prophesied, "Many will come in my name . . . and will deceive many" (Mark 13:6). "Wars and rumors of wars" and "earthquakes . . . and famines" (verses 7–8) would occur. Yet Jesus was careful to explain, when highlighting these specific coming calamities, that "such things must happen, but the end is still to come" (verse 7).

Then our Lord made a succinct, foundational statement declaring one primary sign that had to occur first. He said, "The gospel must first be preached to all nations" (verse 10).

Matthew's description of the same occasion adds further insight. Here we read these words of Jesus:

> "This gospel of the kingdom will be preached in the whole world as a testimony to all nations, and then the end will come."
>
> Matthew 24:14

Note especially the six additional words in Matthew's account: *And then the end will come.*

A careful, word-by-word review of Matthew's record of this vital declaration, looking in particular at the Greek words employed in the text, reveals some amazing insights into precisely how the world might eventually be evangelized, quite literally, prior to Christ's return.

This Gospel

First we note the expression *this gospel.* The word *gospel* comes from the Greek word *euangelion,* which simply means "a good message." *Euangelion* is related to the Greek verb *euangelizo*, meaning "to announce, bring, declare, show a good message or Good News." Here Christ is speaking of "a good message" that in its simplicity declares, shows and announces the existence and reality of His Kingdom.

The message or proclamation need not be complex, nor does it have to be spoken. Its purpose is simply to present the salvation message clearly. That is the Good News!

Of the Kingdom

Then we discover that this "good message" is "of the kingdom"—meaning it concerns the Kingdom of heaven. *Kingdom* is from the Greek word *basileia*, meaning "rule, realm, royalty." It is related to *basileus,* which describes "a foundation of power" or "a sovereign."

Thus, Jesus is speaking of a good message that declares, shows or announces the reality of the Kingdom—which is the realm, royalty and rulership of heaven, the basis of all our power.

Shall Be Preached

Next we discover that this "good message," in simplicity, is to be preached or announced. We first note, of course, the words *shall be*, which declare finality. It will happen—the "it" being the global preaching (or communicating) of this good message of the Kingdom.

The Greek word translated "preached" is *kerusso*, meaning to "proclaim, publish or herald." It does not necessarily mean declaring the Gospel through spoken words, such as from a pulpit, as we traditionally interpret the word *preach*. It actually refers to any form of communicating this "good message," so long as it announces the reality of God's realm and rulership as the basis of our power to be saved.

All the World

Now we discover the scope of the publishing or heralding of this Good News. It will be accomplished throughout "all the world." The Greek form of this word for *all* is *holos*, meaning "whole or complete." As a noun or adverb the word means "altogether, every whit, or throughout."

All appears 5,456 times in the Bible, or an average of almost five times per chapter. Clearly it is one of the most vital words in Scripture. As someone wisely said, "All means all, and that's all all means!" Here it simply means, "In and throughout the whole, entire or complete world."

But we note that this adjective precedes the noun *world*. And it is at this point in our text that we discover something most interesting.

The World

At first glance Christ's use of the expression *the world* seems clear. *All the world* means all the world, right? The Greek word translated "world"—*oikoumene*—means in its most basic sense "inhabited globe" or "populated land." But its makeup from other Greek roots suggests it is not merely our globe as a created and inhabited geological entity that is to be evangelized, but the *individual dwellings* where people live.

In fact, a more careful look at the related roots of *oikoumene* adds even more depth to our definition. The verb *oikeo*, for example, means "to occupy a house; to reside or inhabit." It comes from the Greek word *oikos*, meaning "a dwelling, a family." In some cases it may suggest "a sphere of influence." By using the word *oikoumene*, the Lord might actually have been suggesting that "this gospel" (or good message) that announces the reality and existence of His

Kingdom would be "published and heralded in and throughout the whole globe—dwelling by dwelling, family by family, occupant by occupant."

Frank Kaleb Jansen, global mission strategist and former director of Adopt-a-People Clearing House, says of Christ's use of the word *oikoumene* in Matthew 24:14: "I believe Jesus is actually saying that this gospel of the Kingdom shall be proclaimed to *every home!*"[1]

Jansen appears to have support from W. E. Vine in his *Expository Dictionary of New Testament Words*. Vine suggests the word *oikos* ("dwelling"), which is a root of *oikoumene* when used in such texts as Acts 5:42 (where the disciples are said to have proclaimed the Gospel "house to house"), can actually mean "every home."[2]

Reaching every family or inhabited dwelling makes sense in the completion of Christ's Great Commission because the Lord clearly wants everyone to have access to the Gospel. Recall Peter's declaration that God is "not willing that any should perish, but that all should come to repentance" (2 Peter 3:9, KJV). Paul described the sweep of God's intention when He told Timothy that He desires "all men to be saved, and to come unto the knowledge of the truth" (1 Timothy 2:4, KJV).

As a Witness

The purpose of communicating or heralding the Gospel throughout the whole world, "dwelling by dwelling," is that it might become a witness to all who receive it. The word *witness* used here is from the Greek noun *marturion*, meaning "evidence given" or "testimony." *Marturion* is derived from the Greek word *martus*, meaning "a witness, record, martyr."

This "Good News," the Lord is saying, will be communicated literally to all the inhabited world as "evidence given" to the reality of His Kingdom.

To All Nations

Once again a Greek expression translated "all" is used—but this is a different word from the one employed earlier in the text. Here the expression used is *pas,* meaning "all, any, every, the whole, whosoever, thoroughly." It is an adjective preceding *nations*, making it clear Christ's Good News will reach *every* nation or people group thoroughly before the end comes. Jesus is saying *the whole* of each people group or nation will hear. None will be missed.

Nations

Nations in our text means considerably more than mere geographical entities with boundaries that we think of today when looking at a map of the world. The Greek word used here for nation is *ethnos,* meaning "race, tribe, people, family of people, clan or subclan." Again note the unusual scope of the use of the word *ethnos.* Jesus was speaking of the reality of taking the Gospel not only to all people, right where they live (their *oikos*), but to all "peoples, races, tribes, groupings, clans and even subclans."

Ethnos is the Greek equivalent of the Hebrew *mispahot* used in Genesis 12:3, in which God promised Abraham that through him all the families (*mispahot*) of the earth would be blessed. *Mispahot* refers to "races or subdivisions of ethnic and national groups." Jesus was suggesting here that all peoples everywhere, even in small subclans, will receive the Good News.

Isn't it apparent that for this to happen, the Gospel must be taken literally to where these people live—their *oikos?*

The End Will Come

Only after all the preceding phases occur, according to Jesus, can we anticipate the full culmination of God's plan. Only then will "the end" come.

When our Lord spoke of "the end" ultimately coming, the Greek word used is *telos*, meaning "goal, ultimate objective, conclusion, result or purpose." *Telos* here speaks of Christ's ultimate objective or purpose of His coming Kingdom. *Heko*, translated "come" in our text, means "to arrive" or "come into fruition." Jesus was saying that when all the requirements of the text have been met, His ultimate goal or objective will arrive or come into fruition.

A Summary Paraphrase

There we have it. A detailed and significantly amplified look at all Jesus was saying in Matthew 24:14 might read as follows:

And this good message [that declares, shows and announces the existence and reality] of this Kingdom, which is the realm, royalty and rulership of heaven [the basis of our power], shall be proclaimed, published and heralded in and throughout the whole and completely inhabited globe or land [dwelling by dwelling, family by family, occupant by occupant] as a witness and testimony [of the reality of this Kingdom] to all, any and every race, nation, tribe, people group, clan and subclan, and then [and only then] the ultimate goal, objective and purpose of the Kingdom will fully arrive [and come into fruition].

We might abbreviate that lengthy paraphrase as follows:

This good message from the realm of heaven must be presented personally and completely to every family in every part of the inhabited world—right where people live—and only then God's purpose, as well as the ultimate goal of the Church, will be fulfilled.

The Old-Fashioned Way

Smith-Barney, the prestigious American investment company, tells would-be investors, "We make money the old-fashioned way. We earn it!" They are suggesting that no matter how many gimmicks and trendy ideas other agencies might use to increase investments for their clients, ultimate success will come because their organization works hard. That is "the old-fashioned way."

Such is a principle we might apply to emerging strategies of world evangelization. In the midst of today's explosive technological developments in communication, it is easy to overlook the biblical simplicity with which the early Church employed her strategies of evangelism. Yet if we are ever to measure the completion of the task of taking the Gospel to "every creature" (Mark 16:15, KJV), we must not neglect evangelism the old-fashioned way.

True, technological advances may speed up the process of evangelism significantly, as well as confirm the fruit, but the only truly measurable way to finish the task is the old-fashioned way: *The Church must go where people live.*

In Acts 4 we read about the dramatic results following the healing of a crippled man at the Gate Beautiful (Acts 3:1–10). Because of this miracle, the religious authorities were worried, noting the ever-increasing impact the preaching of the Gospel was having on the city of Jerusalem. After bringing Peter and John before the Sanhedrin (the ruling council) for questioning, the authorities realized that even though these two men were "unschooled, ordinary men" (Acts 4:13), their strange doctrine was spreading. So they conferred privately regarding the matter.

> "What are we going to do with these men?" they asked. "Everybody living in Jerusalem knows they have done an outstanding miracle, and we cannot deny it."
>
> Acts 4:16

The expression *everybody living in Jerusalem knows* is significant. It sets the tone for an even more sweeping declaration from the same group of religious leaders in the next chapter.

There we discover the apostles still proclaiming the Good News boldly everywhere they went. Once again they were arrested and taken before the Sanhedrin for questioning. Angrily the high priest declared, "We gave you strict orders not to teach in this name. . . . Yet you have filled Jerusalem with your teaching" (Acts 5:28).

Note especially the accusation "You have filled Jerusalem with your teaching." What prompted the high priest to use the word *filled*? Was he exaggerating or speaking loosely, or did this religious leader have something more literal in mind?

Part of the answer can be found in the same chapter. The very last verse paints a picture of New Testament evangelism as orchestrated by the early Church leaders: "Day after day, in the temple courts and from house to house, they never stopped teaching and proclaiming the good news that Jesus is the Christ" (Acts 5:42). The King James Version says, "Daily in the temple, and in every house, they ceased not to teach and preach Jesus Christ."

The suggestion here is one of totality—"house to house" (NIV) or "in every house" (KJV)—which might explain why the high priest spoke of Jerusalem as being "filled" with the apostles' teaching. Not a single *oikos* was missed.

Commenting on this passage in his excellent book *That None Should Perish*, Ed Silvoso suggests, "There is only one way to 'fill a city' and that is by doing it house to house."[3]

Simply stated, this is evangelism the old-fashioned way! It is going where people live—to each individual *oikos*.

The Early Church Method of Evangelism

It was this very method of "early church evangelism" that gripped the heart of the founder of the vision that today is known as Every Home for Christ. Jack McAlister was a 22-year-old Canadian pastor with a deep conviction in the power of the printed page. When Jack was a recent Bible school graduate and just married to a beautiful Canadian girl named Hazel, the couple began a weekly radio program they called "The Tract Club of the Air." Originating from Prince Albert, Saskatchewan, the program offered inspirational encouragement and evangelistic literature for witnessing to those who would write in to the program.

Jack sent small packets of tracts to radio listeners who requested them for their own personal witnessing. The listeners, in turn, shared financial gifts, as God enabled them, to help cover the cost of these "paper missionaries" so quantities could be sent to missionaries overseas.

During the earliest weeks of their new vision, Jack became convinced even more of the significance of the printed page in evangelism. A missionary from Africa, Austin Chawner, visited Prince Albert and saw the literature Jack was offering over the radio. This was exactly what was needed in Africa, Austin told him. In fact, he had just purchased a small, manual printing press in Africa, but lacked the paper to print the needed messages.

Then Austin recounted a remarkable story that affected young McAlister deeply.

An illiterate old man from a remote African village had found a small Gospel pamphlet and walked an astounding two hundred miles to find someone who could read the message to him in his language. When he found that person, he asked him to read it slowly for him. The man obliged. Then he said, "Read it one more time." The man read it over and over.

Suddenly the old man grabbed the paper out of the reader's hands, thanked him for taking so much time to read him the message and headed back two hundred miles to his village deep in the bush.

Once there, the old man held up the same Gospel booklet (perhaps upside down!) and began to "read" the message he had memorized from repeated hearings. A crowd gathered to listen. The village was illiterate but had heard about the gift of reading and believed that whatever was printed on paper must be true. Many professed Christ, including the old man, as a result of the Gospel pamphlet.

When Jack heard this testimony and recalled his own experiences of using Gospel literature to win two hundred souls to Jesus in Bible school, he became convinced God would use the printed page to win multitudes to Jesus.

Months later Jack traveled to Africa and confirmed Austin Chawner's testimony about the belief of illiterate Africans in the authority of what was printed on paper. Farmers there would do anything they could to obtain a piece of literature. Then they would cut it into pieces, attach various pieces to sticks, and place a stick in the corners of their fields to ward off evil spirits. Villagers were convinced that the words on these pages, even if they could not read them, held that kind of power.

By then, during the late 1940s, literacy was spreading rapidly across Africa. It was only a matter of time, Jack realized, before there would be at least one reader in each of these African homes. And when that happened, people would truly be ripe for the harvest. They could be reached right where they lived.

The Families of the Earth

Following several years of fruitful ministry in Canada, a Baptist pastor in southern California invited Jack to help bring "The Tract Club of the Air" to what was then one of the largest radio stations, Christian or secular, in the United States. Jack and Hazel prayed about what to do.

Then the Lord spoke to Jack in an unusual way. It was a warm day in the summer of 1951. Jack was meditating on Genesis 12, in which God told Abraham:

> Get thee out of thy country, and from thy kindred, and from thy father's house, unto a land that I will shew thee: And I will make of thee a great nation, and I will bless thee . . . and in thee shall all families of the earth be blessed.
>
> verses 1–3, KJV

Jack was consumed with the passage. Each time he read it, it seemed the message was specifically for him. God was speaking to him directly through Scripture.

So after much prayer, Jack and Hazel were sure God wanted them to move. Within weeks they were on their way, and soon Jack began the weekly radio program in America.

As "The Tract Club of the Air" grew in popularity, Jack's vision for touching the whole world also grew. But there was something special about God's promise to Abraham that Jack could not erase from his mind: *And in thee shall all families of the earth be blessed.* Somehow he was sure this was a promise directly to him. The words *all* and *families* especially intrigued him. He sensed God had a clear plan that soon would unfold, and its focus would be "all families of the earth."

Reaching Every Home

Jack would soon learn what "all families of the earth" meant in his special ministry calling. He soon mobilized his radio listeners to send a million Gospel messages to France, another million to Germany and yet another million to Italy. (Friends would say jokingly of Jack that the smallest number he knew was a million.) It wasn't long before "The Tract Club of the Air" outgrew its name and became a much larger vision called World Literature Crusade, later to be known as Every Home for Christ.

Early in 1953 God led Jack to take his first trip to Japan. When he arrived in Tokyo, it was one of the largest cities in the world. Japan was a vast, unevangelized nation of 83 million people. And two out of every three persons on earth lived in Asia.

Jack met Ken McVety, a respected fellow Canadian he knew only by reputation, who had gone to Japan as a missionary two years earlier. Already Ken had learned to speak Japanese fluently. Together they walked out onto a busy street to ask people if they knew about Jesus.

The first man they spoke with had never heard Jesus' name. Another said he had read about Him in a history book once when he was in the university, but that was all he remembered. An old man wanted to know where this man called Jesus lived.

"We didn't find a single person who knew anything meaningful about Christ!" Jack recalls. Yet this was a country as literate then as the United States or Canada. It was possible to reach the people, Jack was convinced, but he knew it had to be done systematically, family by family, or else millions of people would be missed.

That night Jack and Ken met at Ken's new office flat in Tokyo. There they placed a large map of the city on a typical Japanese *tatami* mat and prayed about a plan to reach every person in Tokyo with the Gospel, as well as in all of Japan. They agreed that if they were to take a Gospel message systematically to every family, it would be necessary to divide the city (and eventually the country) into manageable areas and assign each area to a church. Reaching every home, they were convinced, was the only way to make sure the job got done. It was the only way to measure the results. They also decided that because God loves children, they should print an extra message for each home designed specifically for boys and girls.

By midnight the dream of what they called the "Every Home Crusade" was firmly planted in these two hopeful hearts. And how that dream would come to reality! Within five years every home not only in Tokyo but in all of Japan would be visited.

Today, three additional coverages of the nation have been led by the Japanese Church. More than 396,874 Japanese seekers have sent in response cards included in the literature indicating they have received Christ or that they want to know more about what it means to be a Christian.

In East Asia, carefully tabulated records from Every Home for Christ indicate that 453,813,521 "paper missionaries" have been distributed over the years, the vast majority house to house. If South Asia is added (which includes the vast subcontinent of India), that number swells to an incredible 982,031,802 Gospel messages, or almost one billion. And since the vision has spread elsewhere—to Africa, Latin America, Europe and the Pacific—over two-and-a-half billion "paper missionaries" have been sent out to every country on earth.

What Jack saw as he prayed over the map of Tokyo with Ken McVety was really a simple plan. But if carried to its fulfillment, it could be one of God's key strategies to reach the world for Jesus. Soon other prominent missionary strategists saw the significance of this simple plan that gripped the hearts of Jack McAlister and Ken McVety.

A Veteran Speaks

Few individuals in the last hundred years have had a greater impact on global missions than the late Oswald J. Smith of the renowned People's Church of Toronto, Canada. At a memorial service following the death of Dr. Smith, Billy Graham called him one of the greatest missionary statesmen of our generation. For more than a half-century, literally hundreds of missionaries were supported by the People's Church as a result of Dr. Smith's passionate appeals for missionary advance. Often the church gave three times as much for missions as it kept for its local needs. (Most churches today do well to give ten percent of their income for missions.)

As the veteran pastor was retiring from his many decades of pastoral ministry, he offered this assessment of the ultimate challenge of reaching the whole world, literally, for Jesus:

> For more than 30 years I have prayerfully considered the problem: How can we evangelize the world in the space of one generation? Long ago I was convinced that we could never send out enough missionaries. For a while I gave up hope. But there must be a way. After travel and study in nearly 100 countries, I have come to this conclusion—the only way we are going to be able to carry out the Great Commission, 'Go into all the world and preach the gospel to every creature,' will be by means of the printed page. By the systematic use of the printed page we shall be able to

enter into every home and thus reach every individual with the gospel message.[4]

Oswald J. Smith understood the significance of every-home evangelism, especially through the use of the printed page. He was convinced it was the key to reaching everybody, particularly if methods like audio messages could also be used to reach the illiterate. But the focus must be on everybody. In the early years of the twentieth century, a gifted American Bible teacher, S. D. Gordon, expressed a similar view on what it would take to evangelize the world in a single generation. He wrote the following in 1908:

> The great concern now is to make Jesus fully known to all mankind. That is the plan. It is a simple plan. Men who have been changed are to be world-changers. Nobody else can be. The warm enthusiasm of grateful love must burn in the heart and drive all of one's life. There must be simple, but thorough, organization.
>
> The campaign should be mapped out as thoroughly as a presidential campaign is organized in America. The purpose of a presidential campaign is really stupendous in its object and sweep. It is to influence quickly, up to the point of decisive action, the individual opinions of millions of people, spread over millions of square miles, and that, too, in the face of a vigorous opposing campaign to influence them the other way. The whole country is mapped out and organized on broad lines and into the smallest details.
>
> Strong, intelligent men give themselves wholly to the task, and spend tens of millions of dollars within a few months. And then, four years later, they proceed as enthusiastically as before to go over the whole ground again. We need as thorough organizing, as aggressive enthusiasm, and as intelligent planning for this great task our Master has put into our hands.[5]

Frankly, the Church must become increasingly uncomfortable with the notion of merely reaching as many people as possible with the Gospel before Jesus comes. We should settle for nothing less than "every person," since anything less is outside the will of God (see 2 Peter 3:9). We must employ every means and method to reach this goal, especially the simple, old-fashioned New Testament plan to go right where people live. And it's happening in remarkable ways even as you read this. Let's take a closer look at what God is doing globally through a strategy that takes this Good News right to where people live.

5
Seeds of the Harvest

It was Nepal's monsoon season and the waters of the Daraudi River, usually calm, churned angrily. It would quickly drag into its depths anything caught in its torrents.

As Bishnu Pokhrel stood looking at the raging Daraudi, he told himself it would be better to plunge into the river with his entire family than to face the cruel, ongoing vengeance of his offended Hindu god. Only death, he was convinced, would bring deliverance to his entire household by releasing their lives into another cycle of higher, better existence. He had to persuade his wife to join him. And since circumstances had devastated them both in recent days, he was certain she would agree. Besides, Hindu wives always did what they were told.

Bishnu sighed heavily as he thought of his troubles and how the cruelty of his gods had brought him to the river.

A Black Ram Sacrifice

Bishnu Pokhrel was a strict Hindu born in a typical village of Nepal. He was more fortunate than most, for he was able to attend school for several years, long enough to learn to read and write. But at age eleven Bishnu had to help more on his parents' village farm, so his schooling ended. Most of his time now would be spent tending goats.

During his spare moments Bishnu began to read the Hindu scriptures, often chanting them rhythmically for many hours as he watched the goats throughout the day. This way he was able to memorize lengthy passages of the sacred writings of Hinduism. Every morning after a traditional bath for purification, Bishnu repeated special prayers 108 times. He became a devout Hindu, an example to everyone in the small village.

Through his teen years Bishnu sought work by laboring in the fields of neighbors, gaining a reputation as an able worker. Marriage finally came at nineteen, and later the birth of his first child, a son. Bishnu felt truly fulfilled.

But his joy was short-lived as serious emotional problems developed. One day while climbing a tree to cut food for his animals, Bishnu fell. His injuries brought pain, dizziness, loss of appetite and insomnia. Friends and neighbors, even Bishnu himself, attributed his fall to an evil spirit. In the fleeting times when he could sleep, he was haunted by frightful dreams of painful scorpion bites, tiger attacks and stampeding water buffalo. Was insomnia better than sleep with these torturous nightmares?

Bishnu's parents blamed his young wife, Reka, for their trouble, accusing her of bringing into the marriage some terrible god that had to be appeased with sacrifices. So the Pokhrels, in keeping with their tribal tradition, decided that a black ram had to be killed at the pillar of their house. But no relief came. Finally Bishnu was driven from the family home and forced to live in a cow shed. For months no one visited him, for fear of the strange god bringing about all these disasters.

After Reka gave birth to their second child, a girl, Bishnu's troubles only increased. Now there was another mouth to feed, and Bishnu could not find work. In desperation he called the local *jhankri* (witch doctor). The *jhankri* said that a goat must be killed, and in five days all would be well. The *jhankri* would keep the meat as payment.

Bishnu obliged but nothing changed. So other *jhankris* were called, fourteen in all over the next eighteen months. Each demanded payment, depleting Bishnu's resources. His plight continued to worsen until finally he fell into a semiconscious state that lasted nineteen days. When he came back to full consciousness, Bishnu discovered he had lost everything.

So it was that months later, because of the cruelty of his gods, Bishnu found himself returning to the Daraudi River, this time with his equally despondent wife, tiny son and infant daughter. They felt they had no other choice.

Each parent clutching a child, they walked slowly to the hilly overlook above the turbulent Daraudi. For a few moments Bishnu stood contemplating their fate. Then he said, "It's time!" Both of them, each holding a child, leaped into the raging river below.

A Portrait of Life

Bishnu lost his hold on his son and was tossed violently about for two hundred yards down the treacherous river. Then he was swept onto the shore, where he watched in utter amazement as his entire family, even his infant daughter, washed up safely. Neighbors came running to the water's edge, scolding that it was their fault for "falling" into the river. It was obvious to the villagers that Bishnu and his family had angered the gods.

But some of the villagers took pity on Bishnu and suggested he visit a medical clinic for help. He spent a month at a clinic in Kathmandu, Nepal's capital, but returned in the same physical and mental condition.

Later he traveled to a small mission hospital in the Gurkha district, about a day's walk from their home. There a Christian doctor gave him medication, along with some surprising words: "Don't sacrifice to the idols anymore. That won't wash away your sins." She told Bishnu about Jesus Christ and invited him to accept Jesus' wonderful gift of forgiveness and new life.

He took the medicine but rejected the spiritual advice, which he did not understand. But something inside compelled him to stop offering sacrifices to appease his gods.

Bishnu recovered his health but quickly forgot the message about Jesus.

A decade passed. One day two workers from Every Home for Christ passed through his village visiting every family. Every household was given two Gospel messages, one geared to adults, the other to children.

Bishnu was fascinated by the simplicity of one of the messages, *Are You Happy?* He read the booklet carefully several times, then decided to send in the response card to the address in Kathmandu for additional information. He had vague memories of the doctor's words about forgiveness and wanted to know more about this "Son of God" called Jesus Christ. Hinduism offered nothing like this.

Soon the first of a four-part Bible lesson came, *The Way to a Happy Life.* It provided Bishnu and Reka with an introduction to knowing Jesus Christ personally. Soon another Christian worker traveled to Bishnu's village to give him further nurturing.

So intense was Bishnu's hunger for God's truth that the worker gave him his own personal Bible. Bishnu read it, completed the four Bible lessons and surrendered his life to Christ. Reka followed, as did the children, now almost teenagers.

Weeks later Bishnu and Reka again stood looking into the waters of the Daraudi River. Once again their children were with them. But whereas a decade earlier, a little farther up the river, they had jumped in to die, today they stood at the edge of a more peaceful river, ready for the burial of Christian baptism. The river that a decade earlier had been a picture of death had become a portrait of life.

Bishnu's testimony seems to echo that of Jonah's:

> The engulfing waters threatened me. . . . I sank down. . . . But you brought my life up from the pit, O LORD my God. . . . Those who cling to worthless idols forfeit the grace that could be theirs. But I, with a song of thanksgiving, will sacrifice to you. . . . Salvation comes from the LORD.
>
> Jonah 2:5–6, 8–9

Is Literature Evangelism Effective?

The decision card Bishnu returned to Nepal's office of Every Home for Christ (EHC is actually called Every Home Concern in Nepal) was only one of 3,282 cards received that month. And in the same month, village evangelists visited more than 42,000 families in Nepal.

The every-home evangelism strategy I described in the last chapter has been instrumental in planting well over 2.5 billion printed Gospel "seeds" worldwide, not unlike the small booklet that helped Bishnu and his family come to know Jesus. Since the very first EHC initiative in Japan in 1953, the planting of these seeds systematically, family by family, has brought a remarkable harvest of more than 61 million returned decision cards, each representing in some cases (like Bishnu's) more than one person's decision to receive Jesus. In a recent twelve-month period, more than 23,000 such cards were processed *daily*—or more than eight million in a single year.

Still, many missions strategists continue to treat such evangelism as secondary to other methods. Is the printed page, even when used in a carefully developed, systematic strategy, an inferior or less effective means of communicating the Gospel?

Early in the twentieth century, Charles Cowman, missionary to Japan and founder of the Oriental Missionary Society, read the testimony of a young man who wrote, "I received a Scripture portion, and it was the first time I ever heard that there was a true and living God. I want Him." Cowman became convinced that the printed page would be essential in the ultimate evangelization of the world.

Here is how he described the simple telling of the Gospel story in the early 1900s in Japan:

> From snow-capped Fuji to coral-reefed Loochu, neglected people are coming by the hundreds to the Savior. The pure gospel message accompanied by faith and prayer makes converts anywhere, even where idolatry has held sway for centuries. The greatest success has not been attained by our most skilled preachers. The simple story, told in the simplest way, has brought the multitudes.[1]

Decades later, toward the end of the twentieth century, we must not discount the amazing global increase of literacy that suggests the presence of at least one reader in the vast majority of families in the world. *USA Today* recently reported that the present world average of adults who can read is 76 percent. Even in developing countries it is a remarkable 68.3 percent.[2] Except in some very remote areas, every home probably has at least one reader, maybe more.

And fully half the people of the world, according to Patrick Johnstone in his definitive intercessors' guide *Operation World*, attribute their salvation to the printed page.[3]

Our Most Efficient Medium

The late respected linguist Dr. Frank Laubach, recognized during his lifetime as the world's leading authority on literacy, once wrote, "The basic problems of teaching the world to read have been solved. But there is one unanswered question: What will these millions read?"[4] A grandson of Mahatma Gandhi told an American audience a generation ago, "Missionaries taught us to read, but Communists gave us the books!"[5]

In our generation we have the opportunity to offer the printed message of salvation to every family on earth.

The late Dr. Paul Smith of the People's Church in Toronto, son of the renowned Oswald J. Smith, wrote this in his book *World Conquest*:

> Aircraft, medicine, radio and records, together with many other devices, have certainly multiplied and accelerated the work of every flesh-and-blood missionary. However, with all of these methods combined, the present staff of missionaries, or even a greatly increased staff, could never reach the entire world with the Gospel in our generation. The hope of getting the task completed lies in literature—the Word of God and the Gospel message printed in the language of the people.[6]

Dr. Robert G. Lee, former pastor of the Bellevue Baptist Church of Memphis, Tennessee (later pastored by Dr. Adrian Rogers), said of the printed page:

> Literature can be our most efficient medium of mass communication of the Gospel. Note that I say "most efficient" in terms of the price paid for it, the number of people reached,

and the fact that the message can be read over and over again until it is understood. There is no other method that can compare with literature.[7]

No Bad Days

One of the advantages of printed literature is its repeatable nature. Once while my wife, Dee, and I were spending a morning of prayer and fellowship in the home of Bill and Vonette Bright, founders of Campus Crusade for Christ, Dr. Bright shared his deep conviction about the printed page.

"If God were to give me miraculous, superhuman strength to go to every family on earth and preach for an hour about Jesus," he said, "or if, on the other hand, He permitted me to take a clear, printed message of salvation to every family on earth, there is no question I would choose the latter."

Dr. Bright added, "If I were to preach an hour to every family, there is no doubt that some days I'd probably not do the best job, and many families might not understand my message the first time through. But anointed literature has no bad days. It can stay for months or years, speaking over and over until the Holy Spirit penetrates the heart of the reader."

Such was the case with Bishnu and his entire family. Before he received the booklet from the Christian workers who visited his village, he was preached to by a dedicated doctor at a medical mission. We cannot discount the impact of that simple encounter, even a full decade later. Nor can we discount the fact that the doctor's medical help may have kept Bishnu alive until he finally received Christ. But it was the printed page, which could be read repeatedly, that finally drew Bishnu, and then his family, into an encounter with Jesus Christ.

Some decision cards to EHC, remarkably, have been mailed years after a campaign has concluded. In one year in Japan, for example, 51 decision cards were processed from a campaign in a particular region that had been completed six years earlier. In Africa a decision card came seventeen years after that specific type of literature and decision card had been used in an area!

Are the Conversions Genuine?

So the printed page, when used in a carefully developed, systematic strategy, is not an inferior or less effective means of communicating the Gospel. But how about the written responses to evangelistic literature? Are they as legitimate as the inquirers who respond at a mass crusade or through other means?

I believe there is no difference, if those who respond to literature are truly searching to know Jesus. Paul made it clear in his letter to the Christians at Rome that he was "not ashamed of the gospel, because it is the power of God for the salvation of everyone who believes" (Romans 1:16). The Good News, even when printed very simply in a booklet, can change a life when it is empowered by God's Spirit.

From almost any culture and context, lasting fruit provides ample evidence that conversions through simple house-to-house literature evangelism do last.

Bearing Fruit in China

A young woman we will call Yamiko Kurusawa was born on the Buddha's birthday, April 8—an occasion in Japan of great festivity. They call it *Hana-metsuri*, "Flower Festival," and it is as meaningful to Buddhists as Christmas Day is to Christians. So Yamiko was proud of her birthday, feeling her life must have special meaning that would probably lead to some sort of Buddhist mission.

Yamiko's hometown was Hiroshima, a city famous throughout the world because of the devastation of the atomic bomb dropped in 1945. But Hiroshima is also well known in Japan as the religious center of the Buddhist sect Jodo-Sinshu.

Yamiko's family was serious about Buddhist teachings, partly because some of her relatives were temple priests. Yamiko attended the Buddhist equivalent of Sunday school at the community temple every week until she reached the sixth grade. She was rapidly becoming a devout Buddhist, learning from her mother that Buddhist teaching was the one and only truth.

But when Yamiko entered junior high school, she started reading a Communist newspaper called *Akahata*, meaning "Red Flag." It was mailed regularly to her 22-year-old brother, whom the Japanese Communist Party was seeking to enlist. But the young girl read it with even more enthusiasm than her brother.

"As a naïve teenager," she says, "I was fascinated with Communist ideals, and before long I was sharing these concepts in my classroom as well as at home."

Then one day a young follower of Jesus came to the Kurusawa home. Yamiko answered the door and received an eight-page Gospel pamphlet entitled *A Voice Is Calling You*.

"My heart became warm," she says, "as I took the booklet into my hand and began to read words that have never left my memory: 'Come unto me, those of you who are weary and who carry heavy burdens, and I will give you peace.'"

Yamiko wanted desperately to understand more about this Person named Jesus Christ. Who was He and why did He say those beautiful words? Then she noticed that she could fill out a special card and receive something called a Bible correspondence course. Yamiko had never heard of a Bible.

"When I wrote to the office in Japan," she continues, "I was told about a church that distributed the Gospel messages in my community. God soon gave me courage to attend the church. And a year after receiving the Bible lessons, I was baptized in water at this church, making a public confession of my commitment to Christ. This surprised my family, of course, and they tried to stop me. But I knew my life was completely changed. Because of Christ, I had found what I could not find in Buddhism or Communism."

One day Yamiko was reading John 15:16, where Jesus speaks of choosing His disciples "to go and bear fruit—fruit that will last." Yamiko believed she was called to do just that and decided to become an evangelist.

After high school graduation, several years of work, seminary study and six months of special prayer, Yamiko was convinced the Lord was calling her to China. At that time, 1972, such a mission seemed impossible. China had been a closed door, after all, for many decades. But strangely, within just a few weeks of her call from the Lord, Mao Zedong opened the doors of China to America's president, Richard Nixon.

After years of continuous prayer, Yamiko's church ordained her as their very first missionary to China. Following two years of language training in Hong Kong, Yamiko was recruited by the Teachers University of Xian (pronounced Shian), a major city in China, as a Japanese language teacher. She could live and work in Xian for a year supported by the Chinese government.

As the only Christian among seven foreign teachers on her campus, Yamiko began to be led by God to other believers, some of them secret believers because of government oppression. One of these was a peasant girl from the countryside who served the teachers living in the dorm and whose mother led a Christian meeting in her house every Sunday. What joy it gave Yamiko to provide a large box of Chinese Bibles, brought by Christian couriers, for those believers who for years had had nothing but handwritten portions of Scripture!

Later Yamiko received a two-year contract with the eight-thousand-student Jilin University in Changchun City, Manchuria. At first her attempts to evangelize there met with strong opposition from university authorities. An officer from the notorious Public Security Department, a police agency, even gathered all the foreign students and teachers on campus and warned them not to interfere with government policies regarding religion.

"Please don't forget," he said sternly, "that there is freedom of religion in this country, but not of religious propaganda."

Yamiko Kurusawa knew this spokesman was speaking directly to her. Still, she pursued every possible way to share the Good News with those around her. In December, for example, she decided to hand-deliver Christmas cards to all the Chinese teachers in the Department of Japanese Studies. She was surprised to receive a Christmas card in return from the chairman of the department, and even more surprised to see that he had written a Bible verse inside the card.

Several days later Yamiko visited the professor in his office.

"I went to church for several years when I studied your language in Japan," he explained. "Many times I thought about being baptized." Then he added, "Miss Kurusawa, the Bible is great literature indeed. You should introduce it to your classes. For instance, you could recommend it in your Reading of Japanese Literature class."

Yamiko could not believe what she was hearing. The Public Security official had warned the foreigners that they were forbidden to evangelize, but now she was receiving official permission from the head of her department to use the Bible as a textbook in her classes!

So on Christmas Day Yamiko used her Bible to tell eighty students about the birth of Jesus Christ. She also taught them the Christmas carol "Silent Night." None of the students, representing remote places throughout China, had ever heard "Silent Night," and only four of the eighty had ever heard of Christmas.

Soon Yamiko opened her room for Bible study every Sunday for both Chinese and Japanese students. Many have not only received Christ but have been publicly baptized.

You can see a sparkle in Yamiko Kurusawa's eyes as she refers several decades back to the day a worker from Every Home for Christ came to her doorstep with the Good News. That encounter changed her life, and the seed that took root in her heart has indeed produced "fruit that will last."

6
Winds of the Spirit

Sabir Ali Khan was proud to be a Pathan—a member of a high-caste orthodox Muslim family in India. Many generations earlier his ancestors had come from Kabul, Afghanistan, settling in a town that became known as Tilhar, 260 miles east of India's capital, New Delhi. Although they were originally cloth merchants, Sabir's ancestors soon became farmers, scratching out a difficult existence in the ever-changing climate of the region. But Sabir, a well-educated Pathan, was proud to have risen above all this.

Tilhar, Sabir's hometown, had a population of thirty thousand people, of whom 40 percent were Muslims, 40 percent were Hindus and the remaining 20 percent represented a variety of cults and castes prevalent throughout India.

Sabir often declared he would die for Islam. And what he had heard about Christians caused him to look down on anyone who professed to be one. Years earlier he had heard that two Muslim men from his caste had converted to Christianity and established a Methodist church in Tilhar. But long ago the forty Christian families resulting from those early conversions had moved to bigger cities, and now the church building lay in ruins, so Sabir had never really met a Christian. Still, he despised them.

His Muslim indoctrination had begun when he was enrolled in an Islamic preschool at three years of age. By the time Sabir was eight, he knew many passages of the Koran by heart and had already begun to study other Islamic writings. During all those years, he could not remember missing a single day of saying his prayers or fasting on the required occasions, such as the annual month of Ramadan. Friends and family thought Sabir would surely become a great Islamic spiritual leader someday.

But Sabir became troubled as he moved into his teenage years. Once he read in the *Hadees Tirmizi*, a holy book written by Muslim priests, that during the creation of humankind, Allah had waved his right hand over Adam's back, declaring, "These have I created for heaven," and then waved his left hand, saying, "These have I created for hell." Sabir wondered, meditating on this passage, which hand he had been created from. If it was with Allah's right hand, then no matter how sinful a life he lived, he would still go to heaven. But if he had been created with Allah's left hand, then no matter how good and pure a life he lived, his final destination would still be hell.

For weeks anxiety filled Sabir's heart. And over the next few years, he hungered for true peace and happiness.

A Paper-Wrapped Power Encounter

In 1971, like other 21-year-olds in India who had just finished school, Sabir faced poor prospects for finding a job, so he decided to visit his sister for several weeks. She lived near Lucknow, the capital of Uttar Pradesh, India's northern state.

Her husband worked in management for the Indian railways and owned four racehorses.

One day Sabir sat dejectedly in a park near the outskirts of Lucknow, munching on a small package of peanuts he had bought from a street vendor and contemplating his dissatisfaction with life. As he crunched the last peanut, Sabir noticed that part of the wrapper, which must have been recycled, had printing on it. These words leaped from the paper:

> Peace I leave with you, my peace I give unto you: not as the world giveth, give I unto you. Let not your heart be troubled, neither let it be afraid.
>
> John 14:27, KJV

Sabir did not understand what the word *John*, followed by a strange set of numbers—14:27—meant. But he read more words on the wrapper:

> Come unto me, all ye that labour and are heavy laden, and I will give you rest.
>
> Matthew 11:28, KJV

Rest, true peace, was what he had been seeking!
The paper included still another sentence:

> Him that cometh to me I will in no wise cast out.
>
> John 6:37, KJV

The rest of the message was missing, but an address for India Every Home Crusade in Lucknow appeared at the bottom of the wrapper to which an interested inquirer could write for additional information. So Sabir wrote, asking what the words on the wrapper meant. In less than two weeks he received two booklets on what it meant to be a follower of Jesus, plus the first lesson of a four-part Bible course.

Sabir Ali Khan was so stirred by the literature that he traveled to Lucknow and located the address on the wrapper, where he showed up on the front steps. He spent more than four hours talking to the director, M. M. Maxton, about Jesus and what it meant to follow Him as Lord and Savior. On subsequent visits Mr. Maxton and another EHC leader, Suresh Mathews, provided food and shelter for Sabir when he was in Lucknow, pursuing his intense spiritual hunger.

In 1974, three years after his "power encounter" with the peanut wrapper, Sabir was baptized in water and declared himself publicly a follower of Jesus Christ. Afterward he went straight to his sister and her husband, with whom he was still living, to witness to them for the first time and explain what had happened to him.

Devout Muslims, they became furious, demanding that he recant and even refusing to feed him. During the next few days, Sabir was given nothing to eat but tamarind—a sour fruit used much in India for cooking. His sister and brother-in-law also insisted he find a job.

Sabir found a job pulling a rickshaw for just a few rupees a day, equivalent to less than five cents in today's currency. It was enough to provide him with food. But when Sabir's brother-in-law found out he had taken such a menial job, he beat him with a horsewhip for not trying harder to find a better job, and ordered him angrily to leave their house.

A few days later, God led the young Christian to a good job in a shoe company, where he worked for two years while continuing to study Scripture in his spare moments. His passion to serve Christ grew.

In 1977 Sabir showed up again at the EHC office in Lucknow, inquiring about serving Jesus in a ministry to Muslims. Before long he was working full-time even as he continued his education. In his first few months as a field worker, Sabir led thirty Muslims to Christ. He also met and married a beautiful young woman who, like himself, had been saved out of a strict orthodox Muslim family.

In 1992 Sabir was invited to join Trans World Radio as program producer and evangelist for an Urdu-language program called "Noor-e-Ilahi" (Divine Light) for Muslims. The program, which is still broadcast from the Moscow Center of Trans World Radio every Monday through Friday, touches Muslims and other Urdu speakers across Asia. More than three hundred letters a month come from listeners, most of them Muslims, saying they have received Jesus as Savior.

And it all began with a small portion of a printed message about Jesus wrapped around a handful of peanuts. It was a message the wind of God's Spirit carried to a Lucknow street vendor for its appointment with a youth named Sabir Ali Khan.

A Booklet in the Breeze

In all our strategic planning to reach the world for Jesus, we must never forget that the Lord alone is in charge of His harvest (see Matthew 9:37–38). We are merely His witnesses, His seed sowers. We must plan methodically, of course, and pray mightily. And if we do not want to miss anyone, we must go systematically to where people live. But even then, only God can produce the fruit.

Recall Paul's words to the Corinthian believers—when he was dealing with factions in that church—about seed planting and harvest:

I planted the seed, Apollos watered it, but God made it grow. So neither he who plants nor he who waters is anything, but only God, who makes things grow.

1 Corinthians 3:6–7

If we plant the seeds of the Gospel prayerfully and carefully, God will cause these seeds to produce fruit at the right time:

As the rain and the snow come down from heaven, and do not return to it without watering the earth and making it bud and flourish, so that it yields seed for the sower and bread for the eater, so is my word that goes out from my mouth: It will not return to me empty, but will accomplish what I desire and achieve the purpose for which I sent it.

Isaiah 55:10–11

Some of the seeds may represent a harvest in and of themselves. As someone wisely said, "Any fool can count the seeds in an apple, but only God can count the apples in a seed."

So it was with an eight-page Gospel booklet blown by a humid monsoon breeze toward its divinely appointed destination in Bangalore in southern India. The target: Vasudeva Rao, the eldest son of an orthodox Brahmin family.

Vasudeva had grown up according to strong Hindu tradition. Twice a day he offered his *poojas* (Hindu prayers) to the many deities adorning their home. Some were pictures and some were statues, but all were worshiped. Vasu, following in the footsteps of his father, an ardent Hindu worshiper, sought to attain the special divine enlightenment that Hindus call *Moksha*.

But Vasu was confused as to which god out of the many hundreds, even thousands, he should seek after and worship in order to receive this divine enlightenment. He read many

Hindu scriptures and discovered repeatedly that his gods had committed many sinful actions.

Something within Vasu's conscience would not allow him to accept these beings as real gods. His search for the true God continued. He even prayed a prayer (to whom he was praying, he was not certain): "If there really is a true God, let Him reveal Himself to me." But nothing seemed to happen.

Finally Vasu joined a gang of young criminals, harassing people in Bangalore and indulging in petty crimes. But even this did not last long. Vasu entered into a season of depression and considered ending his life.

Then one day Vasu was walking along a busy Bangalore boulevard. The monsoon breezes, which were beginning to blow briskly, caught a pocket-sized pamphlet and were tossing it playfully in different directions. Suddenly it flew directly toward Vasu and rested quietly at his feet. Vasu retrieved the booklet and stood on the side of the busy road, reading it carefully. The message was simple. It explained how a person could receive Someone called Jesus Christ, the Son of God, as his or her Lord and Savior.

Vasu responded to the message instantly. Even as cars and cattle carts jostled about along the busy boulevard, the young man opened his heart to Jesus.

Vasu's faith in Christ met severe opposition from both family and friends, but he continued to grow in Jesus. He received follow-up materials from the EHC office in Bangalore, including a New Testament, which he soon was devouring every day.

Less than a year later, Vasu applied to work at the EHC Bangalore office, and after careful training became a valued member of the follow-up staff. Hundreds of Hindus who responded to Gospel booklets given home by home received carefully prepared follow-up letters from Vasu. Each was filled with appropriate Scriptures, answering even the most complicated questions. Vasu soon became a popular counselor at seekers' conferences (meetings EHC conducts for new converts) and Christ Groups (the small groups of new believers described in chapter 8).

In the months after joining the EHC ministry and completing the necessary training, Vasu led a remarkable three hundred people to Jesus, most of them Hindus. Of this number he personally baptized 231. To Vasu's special joy, this initial harvest included all his own family members, including his staunch Brahmin parents.

And it all began with a simple multiple-page Gospel message that had been blown his way by a brisk south Indian breeze—and the wind of God's Spirit.

7

Feet with a Mission

There are no easy roads to Isampalli, a tiny village in the Warangal district of Andhra Pradesh, a large state in south India. Anyone wanting to visit that village has to journey many miles from a main road through rugged fields. The region surrounding the tiny town has lost countless lives to famine over many generations. The weather is always hot and water is in scarce supply. The inhabitants of the region are backward socially and economically.

Such was the life Kancha Narasayya was born into 35 years ago. Kancha, the firstborn son, had six brothers and sisters. Raised a strict Hindu, he worshiped trees, animals and snakes. His family's livelihood depended on the constant cultivation of a tiny piece of land. Poverty was their way of life.

The village of Isampalli was located in a district owned by a rich man who ruled like a ruthless king. He treated the villagers as slaves; they rarely tasted the fruits of freedom enjoyed in neighboring regions. But Kancha's parents desperately wanted a better life for their son, so they sacrificed everything to send him to a school in a nearby city. There this Hindu teenager was one of the first people of Isampalli to learn to read and write.

Kancha sought housing at a state-run government hostel. Because he was poor, he received special government grants for his education. In a few years, though he had had no early years of education, he finished high school. But in his classes he was exposed to a variety of philosophies that reminded him of his struggling parents still enslaved by the wealthy landowner of his home district.

Communism soon became the prevailing philosophy of the school, and its influence swept through the region. Eighteen-year-old Kancha was caught up in a radical Communist group known as the Naxalites, a movement begun by university students in a village called Naxalbari in North Bengal, India. Influenced by the philosophy of China's Mao Zedong, Naxalites taught common people that they had to eradicate the rich to become truly free. These Communist radicals carried out raids at night against wealthy people, robbing and killing to achieve their ends.

When Kancha finished school, he was full of enthusiasm and embraced the movement. He agreed to follow its doctrines and spread its vision passionately. Like all good Communists, Kancha declared himself an atheist, decrying the injustices done to the poor as the rich got richer.

In time Kancha moved into the ranks of the junior leadership of the movement. He followed his senior leaders everywhere and learned all he could about effective leadership. A rising star among the Naxalites, Kancha found great satisfaction in serving what he saw as a cause worth dying for.

Before long the impact of the movement intensified. The densely forested hills around Isampalli, where Kancha lived once again with his parents, provided ideal hiding places for young Naxalite rebels mobilized to help in the struggle. Soldiers of the Indian military were sent into the area to arrest those identified as Naxalites.

Kancha's parents heard about the military presence in the area and were afraid Kancha would be arrested. One night they refused to let him leave home. That very night various rebel hideouts were discovered and many of the radicals captured, including most of Kancha's friends. Some were beaten; several were killed. Kancha knew that if he was identified as a leader of the group, he faced a similar fate at the hands of Indian soldiers.

Finding a New Friend

A few days later, two young men visited Isampalli. They were evangelists from India Every Home Crusade, sharing Gospel literature from house to house and giving one booklet to adults and another to younger readers.

Kancha's illiterate parents had no idea what the messages contained. Had these Hindus known the literature was Christian, they would have destroyed it. But the Holy Spirit was at work, and the Narasayyas sensed it was something their son should read.

That night when the young rebel returned home, he read both booklets carefully, but it was difficult for him to grasp the truth of the messages. A war for his soul began to rage. Kancha tossed the booklets aside, determined not to read them again.

The following day his father asked, "What is written on those papers you read last night?"

"Information about a new kind of god," Kancha replied.

"Where is this new god?" asked his father. He thought Kancha meant another Hindu god, of which there were millions.

"I can't really say," said Kancha, and left the house hastily. He had no idea the Spirit of the one true God was at work in his heart.

The next day the youth heard that a close friend of his, another Naxalite, had been killed by soldiers. A large memorial service was held in remembrance of the young man, whose body was cremated Hindu-style amid burning sticks. Kancha had considered his friend wise, well educated and morally upright, and he returned home that night deeply depressed and unable to sleep. Emptiness flooded his heart. Slumped on a chair, he thought about the problems of life and the seeming lack of solutions to human suffering.

Suddenly Kancha saw the two Gospel booklets resting on a table across the room. He made his way to the table, staring intently at their titles: *From Darkness to Light* and *Do You Want a Good Friend?* The booklet about finding a good friend, in the wake of the death of Kancha's close friend, captured his interest. He had read it several times two days earlier. But he could not grasp how this Person called Jesus Christ, who lived so long ago, could be his special Friend.

Even so, he filled out the accompanying response card and sent it to the Every Home Crusade office in Secunderabad. In less than two weeks Kancha received four Bible lessons, which he soon finished, and received a graduation certificate, along with a New Testament.

He set the Bible aside without reading it. He still had many unanswered questions about life and a continuing sense of emptiness.

The battle for Kancha's soul continued for six months. The two EHC field workers who had first come to his village continued to visit regularly to talk with this young man—the only person from Isampalli to respond to the Gospel. In fact, no Hindu in any village in the region was known to have accepted Jesus. Still, the Christian workers counseled Kancha about life, death and salvation through Jesus Christ. Once, they stayed for several days, talking to him continually about the ways of God.

Victory finally dawned on the battlefield of Kancha's heart. The young Communist leader opened his heart to Jesus and received Him as his Lord and Savior.

The process of conversion had been slow in Kancha's life, but the change was dramatic. He could not contain his joy. Soon each member of his family surrendered to Jesus Christ. The Narasayya home became a center for evangelism for the village (the first village in the region known to have had a Hindu accept salvation in Christ) and the surrounding area. Many in Isampalli found Jesus as Lord and Savior.

As Kancha studied God's Word, he recognized his need to be baptized. He also wanted to change his name, feeling it had too many ties to his Hindu past. He had read in the gospels about Christ's disciple named Nathanael and wanted to be like him. When the day of his baptism arrived, he invited other recent converts to join him, and 25 villagers responded. He entered the waters of baptism as Kancha Narasayya but came up shouting, "I will be Nathanael!"

Soon Nathanael set about to visit every home in hundreds of villages dotting the countryside around Isampalli, and throughout the vast Indian state of Andhra Pradesh, sharing how they, too, could meet his good Friend. He felt as if God had given him "feet with a mission." Every step he took seemed to be driven by the words of Scripture:

"How beautiful are the feet of those who bring good news!"

Romans 10:15

Crusaders for Christ

The Christian workers who took the Gospel to Isampalli are two modern-day soldiers on the front line of the battle for souls. The work of reaching every home with the Gospel in remote areas would be impossible without such foot soldiers willing to take the Good News where others have not been. The conversion of Nathanael, who himself became a pioneer missionary with Every Home for Christ, took place only because two other young men were bold enough to enter his troubled region. Nor did they stop after one visit. They came again and again.

Although most systematic, home-to-home EHC evangelism initiatives use Christian volunteers, it became clear in the early years of the ministry that carefully trained, full-time crusaders would be essential to reach remote places where volunteers simply could not go. Often these "pioneer missionaries," as they came to be called, face beatings or even death as they spread the Good News of Jesus. These workers, especially in Hindu or Muslim lands, may have their literature seized and burned while their luggage or backpacks are thrown down steep mountainsides or into raging rivers.

Not long before Nathanael came to Christ, one of the field workers evangelizing in his area was stripped naked and tied to a tree for almost a full day. Only God's protection kept deadly animals away. Late that night he was brutally beaten and finally released.

A postman in nearby Karnataka, India, observed about these crusaders for Christ: "I am amazed at the faithfulness and sincerity with which these young men go about their work. I have been assigned just three villages in the area, and sometimes I'm not even faithful in taking the mail to all of them. But these young men go to many more villages than I do, and they do so with great joy."

Pioneer missionaries are full-time personal evangelists who visit literally hundreds of homes in an average week. They are usually young men, although young women are permitted to participate in areas where it is acceptable culturally and where they will not be endangered. A pioneer missionary must be in good health because of the tremendous physical hazards associated with the work. He or she must possess above-average knowledge of the Bible and must often counsel new converts in unusually remote areas where no churches have ever existed. The average worker preparing for Every Home for Christ initiatives undergoes four to six weeks of intensive training to become familiar with the overall work of the ministry and to be equipped spiritually for the task.

Each pioneer missionary carries only enough equipment for basic needs like eating and sleeping. Often nightly meals are cooked over a campfire alone or with a partner. Usually he or she is equipped with a bicycle. (In many countries very few other forms of transportation are reasonably available.) It is not uncommon in some nations to see a pioneer missionary carrying a bicycle on his or her shoulders while crossing a river or traversing a rugged hill.

An average EHC field worker can reach as many as two hundred families in a single day. But I also have met such workers in the South Pacific who traveled by boat two or three weeks over rugged seas just to visit a tiny island with only eleven families. In other regions, where the population is more dense, a pioneer missionary may visit considerably more families per day. They work faithfully five or six days a week to make sure no home is missed. In the Mount Everest region of Nepal, teams of workers were flown in by helicopter and left for days to visit Sherpa villages before being picked up and flown out again. No known village was missed.

Many EHC pioneer missionaries, like Nathanael, are converts of the very ministry they now serve full time. They recognize the need to go to the most remote places. After all, if someone had not bravely come to them, they might never have known of Christ's love.

Pedaling for Jesus

Joseph Gambo, who lives in the Rift Valley of Kenya, is just such an example. He came to know Christ through a simple printed Gospel message when workers visited his remote village more than two decades ago. The young African picked up the booklet titled *He Wants to Be Your Friend* and read about Christ for the first time. That very day he gave his heart to Jesus.

Joseph soon felt a passionate desire to tell others about Jesus. So he wrote the distant EHC office in Kenya asking for quantities of literature, which he promised to distribute systematically from home to home in surrounding villages. Soon Joseph became an unofficial pioneer missionary. He rode his bicycle over rough roads, through heavy rains and under the scorching African sun—sometimes pedaling for Jesus more than two hundred miles in a given month.

Because Joseph was the only known Christian evangelist working in the entire area, it became clear that the amazing spiritual fruit growing throughout the region was the result of Joseph's labors. In just 36 months an estimated seventeen thousand Africans came to faith in Christ in Joseph's region as a direct result of his efforts.

Like Nathanael, he had feet with a mission.

Walking Around His World

Daniel Soeharto from Central Java, Indonesia, converted from Islam after reading a single twelve-page Gospel booklet.

He joined a group of seven believers in his small village, then entered an EHC training program to become a full-time church planter. Finally Daniel began a remarkable ministry that, by the time I met him on a memorable journey to Central Java while researching for this book, had touched literally hundreds of thousands of families.

For fourteen years Daniel distributed Gospel literature home to home averaging one village a day, five to six days a week, 48 weeks a year. He has evangelized more families than any worker I have ever met.

Daniel kept written records for every village he visited. These records show that with an average of three hundred homes per village and five persons per home, Daniel has provided reasonable access of the Gospel to about 1,500 people a day, or 360,000 people each year (counting 240 days of ministry). Multiply this total by fourteen years of service, and you can see that this dedicated worker may have taken the message of Jesus Christ to an astounding 5,040,000 people (in about a million households).

And because the EHC ministry in Indonesia yields about a 3 percent harvest of decision cards per home from its home-to-home initiatives (double or triple that of many parts of the world), Daniel may be responsible for more than 30,000 people pursuing a knowledge of Christ out of the 1,008,000 Indonesian households he visited. (Further, because these cards often represent more than one decision per household, the actual number of individual decisions may be much higher.)

To accomplish this incredible task, Daniel trekked to distant and remote areas of Central Java. Sometimes buses were available to transport him to certain areas, but he traveled mostly by foot or bicycle. He walked an estimated seven miles a day, or a minimum of 35 miles a week. So we can calculate that, traveling 48 weeks per year, he walked an amazing

23,520 miles in fourteen years. That is equivalent to walking completely around the world at least once in order to tell others about Jesus.

Talk about feet with a mission!

Feet of Faith

Often these "feet with a mission" find themselves taking unusual steps of faith that produce much joy. Recently, for example, an EHC Solomon Island worker named Sakiusa prepared a list of supplies that the EHC base on their remote island needed to sustain its outreach. The list included office stationery, kitchen utensils, household items and various hard-to-find farming implements. The total cost: two thousand dollars. Sakiusa took a boat to the distant capital city of Honiara on Guadalcanal Island, trusting God would meet their needs—though he had no idea how. He had spent his last dollar for his boat fare.

When he arrived at the wharf, a young man in a government van who had heard Sakiusa was coming was waiting for him. Having no idea about the list of needed items, he informed Sakiusa that he had brought several pieces of equipment for the base that he thought Sakiusa might need. They compared lists and found that about half of the items needed so desperately had already been purchased and were already waiting in the van! Then the young man drove Sakiusa to where he was to lodge for the evening. It was at an inn owned by Christians who provided him free lodging.

That night Sakiusa received a surprise gift from a foreign visitor of twelve hundred dollars in cash. It was exactly what he needed. He did the rest of the shopping the next day, obtaining every item on the list. He was even able to buy a large rug for the floor of the base office and purchase airfare back to his home island.

Sakiusa had set out for Honiara with only a list of needs and a heart of faith. Now he was returning with boxes of blessings and a heart of joy.

Similar was the joy experienced by a young EHC worker in Fiji traveling to a distant city to fulfill that day's assignment. The bus fare was $2.05, but he lacked even a single cent for the journey.

Lord, he prayed, *touch one of Your children who is here in town to bring my bus fare to me.*

He even told God the exact amount. Then he waited and watched. No one came.

He waited a little longer. Then he sensed the Lord speaking: *When do you really need the money—now or when you board the bus?*

The answer was obvious. He did not need the money until he boarded the bus. So the worker promptly headed for the central bus station. He hoped another believer would see him as he walked along and ask if he had any needs.

But he soon arrived at the bus terminal, still with no fare. Passengers were already boarding, though the bus driver had not yet come.

Another thought came to him: *Exactly when do you need the fare—now or when the driver gets on the bus?*

Again the answer was obvious. He did not need the $2.05 until the bus driver arrived. So he boarded the bus and made his way to a seat near the back. He knew the bus driver would get on shortly and begin collecting the fares.

So he prayed once again, *Lord, I'm on the bus now, and soon the driver will come to start collecting the fares. I am still waiting for my bus fare. Please send someone soon to bring me the money.*

Several minutes passed while the worker sat anxiously by the window. In a moment the bus driver boarded and started the engine to move the bus forward to allow another bus to depart.

Suddenly it happened. Just as the bus began moving, someone called the evangelist's name through the open window. A Christian brother had seen his old friend from the other side of the street and dashed over to ask him where he was going. The evangelist explained he was heading to a particular city for ministry.

Quickly the friend reached into his pocket, pulled out a two-dollar Fijian note and handed it to the young worker.

"Here," he said, "buy yourself something to eat along the way."

The worker's heart was flooded with joy, although he was still five cents short.

"My brother, God has brought you here at this exact moment to help provide my fare," he responded joyfully. "I've been asking God to provide a miracle because I had no money when I got on the bus."

"How much is the total fare?"

Only then did the evangelist admit he still lacked a nickel; whereupon his friend, God's special agent, took an additional dollar note from his pocket and handed it to this faith-traveler.

"Here," he shouted over the roar of the bus engine. "This will help pay the rest of your fare."

Another mission—another miracle. And oh, the joy of it all! The Fijian worker's faith and his feet with a mission were facilitating the spread of the Good News of Jesus Christ across that island nation of the Pacific Ocean.

And especially exciting: This pioneer missionary knew that the end result of his steps of faith would mean the planting of many new churches—a vital fruit of this Every Home for Christ strategy that we will read about next.

8
Graveyard of Siberia

Olga rubbed her tired eyes and pondered her next words in answering the essay question about the early days of the Bolshevik Revolution. The exam had just begun, but already her mind was wandering. She had traveled many hours from the remote Siberian city of Magadan, on Russia's far eastern coast, where she had served for several years as a professor of Marxist philosophy at the University of Magadan.

Magadan, a city of one hundred thousand, is known to Russians as "the graveyard of Siberia" because more than nineteen million Soviet citizens are buried there. It was here that Stalin and other Soviet leaders most often sent dissidents, criminals and other perceived troublemakers for a life of exile or, not infrequently, execution. Magadan is also called "the Siberia of Siberias," because for half of the year the city is almost completely isolated by Arctic winter. Even planes cannot fly in because of the severe winter weather, and the sea between Magadan's coast and northern Japan freezes over, making shipping impossible.

Olga had come to accept life in Magadan, however, and had proven a gifted professor of Marxist-Leninist philosophy at the university. Now, as required by her school, she had flown across the Sea of Okhotsk, over Sakhalin Island, to the city of Khabarovsk to take an exam that would upgrade her credentials. She had no idea of the dramatic, even supernatural change that was about to take place in her life.

The young philosophy professor picked up her pencil and tried to write another sentence. Suddenly, for apparently no reason, a strange thought flooded her mind: *I have to find God.* Atheists usually do not think such thoughts, and Olga had been an atheist all her life.

She tried to write another sentence, but her urge to find God only increased. Soon this unusual feeling was accompanied by a sense of anxiety. Olga had to do it *now*. The urge simply would not wait.

Her heart raced. The feeling turned to near-panic. She could not explain it, but she laid her pencil on the test pages and jumped to her feet. Before the startled presiding instructor could open his mouth, Olga dashed from the room, rushed down the stairs and into the street.

I must find God.

The one place Olga thought to go was to the Orthodox church in the center of Khabarovsk. She had heard only negative stories about the Church in Russia, but it was the only place she knew she might find God.

She found the church quickly with its traditional, onion-shaped dome rising high against the gray Russian sky. Darting into the ornate sanctuary, its walls adorned with glistening icons, she was met by an Orthodox priest.

"I must find God!" she burst out.

The priest stared at her stoically, then handed the obviously distraught woman several candles.

"Light these," he said, "then kiss some of the icons hanging along the walls."

Olga knew instinctively this was not the answer she sought.

"No," she informed the priest abruptly. "I didn't come to find religion. I came to find God."

With that she turned and rushed from the church.

A few minutes later, out on the street, she saw, to her amazement, a large poster attached to a decaying brick wall. It said in Russian that an American "evangelist" (a new word to her) was in Khabarovsk that week to tell people how they might find God. The poster included the address and times of the meetings. Unbelievable!

That night the young professor located the old Communist hall rented for the evangelistic meetings. Every aspect of the service fascinated her, including the lively singing and well-prepared message about what it meant to be a follower of Jesus Christ. She was one of the first to respond to an invitation to receive Jesus as Lord and Savior.

Olga never returned to the exam room to finish her test. So startling was her transformation, in fact, that she knew she could never teach Marxist philosophy again.

When she arrived back in Magadan several days later, she went to the head of her department at the university, intending to resign.

"I can no longer teach Marxist-Leninist philosophy," she announced.

"Why not?" the department head asked tersely.

Olga recounted her unusual experience in Khabarovsk and explained that she had found God.

"It's not necessary for you to cease teaching Marxist-Leninism," he objected.

"But I cannot teach something I don't believe in."

Then he explained that there was such a shortage of teachers of her caliber in Magadan that he simply did not want to lose her. She insisted she could no longer teach Marxism.

"What would you be willing to teach?" he asked.

"I can teach the Bible as philosophy," she answered haltingly. "That I can believe in."

To Olga's amazement her supervisor agreed.

"That will be fine," he said. "You may teach the Bible as philosophy, as long as you stay in the university."

Thus began a remarkable chain of events in the teaching career of this young philosophy professor. Within six months Olga had led sixty of her students to Jesus Christ and, in addition to conducting her usual classes, met with them in weekly Bible teaching sessions.

Soon several of Olga's students came to her.

"We need a full-time pastor," they said.

"I'll try to find someone suitable," she replied.

"Our group has already discussed it," said the students. "We all agree you should be our pastor."

After considerable encouragement, Olga finally agreed, and a church was born.

Interestingly, only a few months later, Paul Iliyn, then regional director of Every Home for Christ for the Commonwealth of Independent States (CIS), visited Magadan and heard Olga's unusual testimony. He had come to begin an every-home evangelism and church-planting campaign in far eastern Siberia and needed a place to begin a Bible school to train young church planters. Olga quickly volunteered her church, and within six months 26 students had enrolled full-time in the training center.

Filling Up Their Town

The Bible school in Magadan was a sister school to one Paul Iliyn had established in Kiev, Ukraine, not long after the breakup of the Soviet Union. The need for trained leaders was especially strong in the old Soviet republics. For seventy years they had been bound in atheism, with seminaries and Bible schools closed and sometimes destroyed. The result: a tremendous shortage of qualified church leaders and thousands of smaller towns and villages with no evangelical church of any kind. Carefully equipped men and women were needed to go into these towns, reach every family with the Gospel and plant churches with those who responded. Paul knew that for this to happen, they needed Bible training schools to produce able church planters.

By 1993 the training center in Kiev, called St. James Bible College, had established two hundred young men and women deep in God's Word and trained them to become evangelists, pastors and church planters (with the assistance of Paul Iliyn's home church, The Church of the Highlands, in San Bruno, California, and Kay Arthur and her Precept Ministries staff of Chattanooga, Tennessee). In 1995 the second training center was established in Olga's church in Magadan (also with the help of The Church of the Highlands and Precept Ministries).

One of the very first church planters from St. James Bible College was Vasily Dektorenko. Barely in his twenties, Vasily was convinced that he and his brother, Alex, who lived not far from Kiev, could "fill up" their town with the Gospel, house to house on weekends, even while Vasily continued his studies at the Bible college on weekdays. So he approached the school administrator.

"Sir, do I need to complete an entire year of training before I can start reaching people with the Gospel in my hometown?"

"It is essential that you complete your training," the director explained, "if you are to become an effective pastor. But there's nothing wrong with putting into practice now what you have already learned."

So Vasily and Alex began an every-home evangelism campaign the very next weekend in their hometown of Zhitomir.

Soon they were on their way to sharing the Good News of Jesus with every home in Zhitomir. With the help of a few volunteers, the brothers visited more than 25,000 families over the first few weeks. Each family was given not only a Gospel message and response card, but a special invitation to attend a new church being started in the city.

On the day of the first church service, the two young brothers were astonished to find nearly four hundred people gathered from throughout the city. The former Communist hall they had rented was packed. There were no deacons, elders or ushers, and the people present had never attended a church in their lives. Vasily began by asking how many had come to the meeting to learn more about Jesus Christ. Everyone raised his or her hand. Then Vasily asked how many wanted a New Testament. Again, every hand went up.

Thankfully, about a month before the first meeting, a shipment of New Testaments in their language had arrived from International Bible Society in America. Praise God! Everyone was given his or her own New Testament. It was an instant church of four hundred new believers.

But the growth had just begun. Within two years the congregation consisted of 46 separate discipleship groups, called Christ Groups, with a total membership of at least three thousand.

The concept of a Christ Group had grown out of necessity many years earlier in the ministry of Every Home for Christ, when new believers were coming to Christ in areas with no churches of any kind.

The Christ Group Phenomenon

Christ Groups like the ones in Zhitomir, Ukraine, represent the answer to a significant challenge Every Home for Christ faced in 1975.

That year EHC completed its first nationwide every-home coverage of the vast nation of India, then with an estimated 550,000 villages. The ten-year task had involved as many as eight hundred full-time evangelists and many thousands of volunteer workers during any given month. The fruit was encouraging: 1,250,258 Indians, mostly Hindu and Muslim, sent in decision cards—the majority of which (about 67 percent) indicated that the senders had prayed to receive Jesus Christ as Lord and Savior. The remaining 33 percent wanted additional information about what it meant to receive Christ. Of the latter group, more than half found Christ while studying the EHC Bible correspondence course.

Naturally, the process of discipling so great a number seemed almost impossible, even though every person responding was already enrolled in a well-prepared, four-lesson Bible course. About 90 percent of the responses came from people who lived in tiny villages, hamlets and even moderate-sized towns with no Christian church of any kind to provide adequate nurturing and fellowship. What would happen to these new believers, EHC workers wondered, even if they completed the Bible course successfully? It seemed almost criminal, spiritually speaking, not to provide some means of ongoing follow-up to assure that these new converts would become functioning members of a local church. But how could that happen in places where no organized group of believers existed?

The answer came as the result of hundreds of hours of prayer and discussion regarding the preservation of the harvest.

The Christ Group Defined

Christ Groups—such as the ones begun by Vasily and Alex Dektorenko in the brand-new church in Zhitomir—are small cells of new believers formed as a result of home-by-home evangelism and established primarily in areas with no Bible-believing congregations.

The concept of a Christ Group is based on a pattern originated by Jesus—"Where two or three are gathered together in My name, I am there in the midst of them" (Matthew 18:20, NKJV)—and implemented by Paul in his relentless missionary travels. Paul sought to form and sustain cells of new believers right where they lived so they could communicate with one another and enjoy fellowship in prayer and Bible study (see Romans 16:5 and 1 Corinthians 16:19).

The late Dr. Jim Montgomery, writing in his book *DAWN 2010: A Strategy for the End of the Age*, strongly affirms the need for Christ Groups. The leader of the DAWN strategy (to "Disciple A Whole Nation" through saturation church planting), Montgomery refers to Paul's explanation of the process involved in proclaiming the Gospel: "We proclaim [Christ], admonishing and teaching everyone with all wisdom, so that we may present everyone perfect in Christ" (Colossians 1:28).

Believers with a heart for the lost, says Dr. Montgomery, realize we must proclaim the Gospel to everyone by every means available. But, the missiologist adds:

> According to this verse [Colossians 1:28], we also want to admonish and teach *everyone* so that *each* may be presented perfect in Christ. This can happen only when new believers are gathered in a teaching, growing, worshiping, discipling environment: a church. And only when there are churches *everywhere* in a nation and people group can such a setting be made available for *everyone*.[1]

The Christ Group Purpose

Where there are already solid evangelical churches in an area, EHC workers always encourage new believers to join one. They also ask the local churches to visit and nurture the new believers. But they organize Christ Groups for new believers in places where no churches exist to nurture them.

Each local EHC office has some idea of how far along a new believer is spiritually by his or her response to the Bible lessons or by letters he or she has written. Then a field evangelist is sent to an area where these new believers live and uses this information, while meeting with them, to designate initial leaders for each group.

Although the primary purpose of a Christ Group is to provide nurturing where it is otherwise unavailable, groups are also formed in some places like the old Soviet Union where some evangelical churches, because of legalism or traditionalism, do not welcome new believers.

The Christ Group Plan

Each Christ Group meets once or twice a week in various members' homes, spending about two hours at each meeting. The first forty minutes are devoted to Bible study, the next forty minutes to sharing victories and problems of various members, and the final forty minutes to prayer.

Critical to a group's success is the careful attention by the field evangelist who first formed the group. Ideally, twice each month the worker visits each Christ Group in his or her assigned region, meeting first privately with the leader of the group, then with the entire membership (depending on each local situation). The purpose: to guide or offer help in situations beyond the spiritual understanding of these relatively new believers.

After twelve months of intensive, twice-monthly follow-up, the Christ Group begins to function on its own. If it grows into a sizable congregation, it is encouraged to affiliate with a larger evangelical denomination. (Many Christ Groups, such as ones in Indonesia and Fiji, have grown into sizable independent local churches that later chose to form their own fellowship of churches.)

The Gospel in Gomolong

But can house-to-house evangelism using something as simple as Gospel literature actually result in the planting of churches? I sought the answer to this question firsthand in the world's most populated Muslim land, Indonesia, when I visited there while writing this book.

My adventure began with a 24-hour, twelve-thousand-mile journey by jumbo jet to the other side of the world, followed by a long, bumpy ride over the rocky, hilly terrain of Central Java with our then-director for Indonesia Every Home Contact, Romy Romulo. I had made the journey to see with my own eyes the unusual fruit of a single Gospel booklet that had begun a chain reaction resulting in the planting of the only church in this remote Muslim area.

Romy and I found ourselves in a town called Somondomore, about fifty miles outside the city of Yogyakarta. Somondomore is an Islamic community of about 3,500 people, with houses scattered across the rugged, mountainous region.

High on the hillside before us, for everyone in the village to see, stood a beautiful church building constructed by the new Christians who now worshiped there. Standing beside Romy and me was a young pastor and EHC field evangelist, Daniel Soeharto, the convert from Islam I described in the last chapter who walked an amazing 23,520 miles in fourteen years (the equivalent of walking completely around the world at least once) in order to tell other Indonesians about Jesus.

Soon I would be addressing the modest but growing congregation of that church, explaining why I had journeyed from half a world away just to see what God was doing in their village. I saw their joy and realized I was witnessing the amazing results of what can happen in "the uttermost parts of the earth" when someone is courageous enough to take the Gospel where others have never gone.

But first I asked Romy how this church came to be. He smiled and explained that it had actually begun about fifteen years earlier. That was when Daniel Soeharto lived in a distant village called Gomolong.

He had been visited there by two young EHC evangelists who were taking the Gospel house to house throughout the region. They visited every home in Gomolong that day, giving out simple Gospel presentations for adults and children. Neither of the two booklets was more than twelve pages long.

Nineteen-year-old Daniel read both messages with careful intensity. Although he had grown up in a strict Islamic culture, he was fascinated by these messages. In fact, it seemed to him that a brilliant light shone on each word as he read. When he finished, he prayed the brief prayer suggested at the end of the booklet and received Jesus Christ, the only Son of God, as his Lord and Savior.

Others in Daniel's small village were reading the same messages that day. In fact, by the time Daniel finished filling out the decision card accompanying the booklet, at least seven others in his village had done the same. The Gospel had come to Gomolong.

Within a few days the Every Home for Christ office in Jakarta received those decision cards and followed them up by sending the first lesson of a four-part Bible correspondence course. After Daniel finished the fourth lesson in the course, he wrote the EHC office for additional help and was told that a Christ Group would be forming in his village. Daniel joined the group for its very first meeting.

Several months later he heard about a newly formed Christ Group training center in his region of Central Java, where people who had received Christ in the village campaigns were being trained as full-time workers to reach even more villages. In spite of the objections of his Muslim family, and despite the rejection he had experienced from his friends and community, Daniel applied for training at the center and was accepted.

In the months that followed, Daniel led the members of his family one by one to Christ—the two Gospel booklets delivered to his home producing even more fruit.

Following a year of training, Daniel became a full-time Christian worker with the Indonesia Every Home Contact outreach. He knew that all the villages he would visit in the days ahead were Muslim. He also knew the opposition faced by any Muslim who became a Christian. But Daniel had great hope in his heart, because he now knew the power of God for salvation.

Little did he realize how much of Central Java he would visit, sharing the Good News of Jesus Christ with as many as five million people over the following decade and a half.

A Tale of Two Seeds

Years later I stood with our Indonesian EHC director at the time, Romy, and with Daniel as we gazed at the beautiful church in Somondomore. It touched me that Daniel could still remember the titles of the two booklets that had brought the Gospel to him: *He Wants to Be Your Friend* and *How to Enjoy Life to the Fullest*. And his story made me consider the power of the printed page to change lives.

How, I asked Romy, had Daniel come to be the pastor of this church? And had he actually planted it himself while continuing the work of taking the Gospel to so many of the neighboring villages?

Then I heard the rest of the story. A full six years before Daniel received the seed of the Gospel at his home in Gomolong, another EHC evangelist was distributing identical seeds in Central Java. Because no village was to be missed, he eventually reached the Muslim village of Somondomore— the village in which we now stood—where, to his knowledge, no Christian witness had ever come. He distributed the Good News of Jesus to every home and, whenever possible, gave a personal witness, although no one showed any interest.

But one old man in the village had been touched by the simple message. Mr. Huparman read his booklet repeatedly. Then one night, with great courage, he filled out the decision card and mailed it to the EHC office in Jakarta. Mr. Huparman was the only person in the entire village to respond.

Soon he received the first lesson of a Bible correspondence course titled *The Way to a Happy Life* and completed it. A second lesson came, then a third. By the fourth and final lesson, Mr. Huparman (but not his wife) opened his heart to Christ. Upon finishing the course, the old man wrote a beautiful testimony describing how Jesus had changed his life.

For several years he continued to be the lone Christian in the village, worshiping Jesus secretly. But a desire for fellowship with other believers flooded his heart, so he wrote the EHC office asking if someone could come to his village and help him grow in Jesus as well as tell others about Him. Daniel Soeharto, who by then had found Christ in Gomolong and finished his Christ Group training, was assigned by the EHC office to visit the village.

When Daniel arrived in Somondomore, Mr. Huparman met him with great enthusiasm. Although he was the only convert in the village, they decided to begin a Christ Group. Mr. Huparman invited one other person, a man named Warsito who was sympathetic to Christianity because of the changes he had seen in Huparman's life.

Within days Warsito gave his heart to Christ, and a tiny Christ Group of just two people (three when Daniel was present) began. For many weeks the number stayed the same. Meanwhile, Daniel continued to visit towns and villages throughout the area, with periodic stops at Somondomore.

More than a year passed. Then they decided to hold an Easter Sunday meeting and invite everyone in the village. Amazingly, scores of villagers came and several received Christ as Lord. Soon the number of converts grew to almost fifty adults and seventeen children. Mr. Huparman's wife finally became a believer. The church was well established, and soon the offerings of many members of the Christ Group enabled them to build a new sanctuary to adorn the highest hill overlooking Somondomore.

When I visited the village, the Somondomore congregation had a missionary vision to reproduce themselves in other villages of the region. Members proudly showed me their maps and five-year plan to plant at least two churches a year for the next five years in neighboring villages.

I marveled at the grace of God and how this church had begun out of two simple, printed Gospel seeds—one planted in the heart of Daniel Soeharto years earlier in the distant village of Gomolong, and one in the heart of Mr. Huparman in Somondomore. God was clearly at work among the previously unreached peoples of Central Java, and the planting of many new churches through the Every Home for Christ vision was the result.

9

Captives for Christ

Ramudu of Tumella, India, was an untouchable, but not because he fell into that particular Indian caste. Ramudu was an untouchable because, like many others in various nations who are put into prison, he fell into a unique category of the unreached.

Ramudu was six feet three inches tall and weighed 170 pounds—an exceptional physique for an Asian. He terrorized the villagers of Tumella. Officially he murdered five people; unofficially, nobody knows—nobody dares to say. He was known to have flown into a rage and grabbed a man by his legs, turning him upside down and smashing his head on the rocky ground until he was dead. Over the years Ramudu was incarcerated various times for his crimes and became a terror even within the prison walls. He was motivated by hatred, anger and vengeance.

While serving a prison term for murder (he had somehow escaped the death sentence), Ramudu was visited by two EHC field evangelists who were calling on every dwelling in the area and sharing a printed introduction to Jesus as Savior. The prison warden granted permission for these workers to visit every cell and give every inmate a Gospel message.

But Ramudu did not read the booklet.

On his release, Ramudu was charged with another murder and sent to a prison in South Central India near the city of Hyderabad. This time it appeared there was no avoiding the death sentence.

This prison, interestingly, was visited by one of the same Christian workers Ramudu had seen a year earlier. This amazed him. He was impressed by the persistence and compassion of these people. No one else had come even once to encourage him or offer hope, while this worker had visited twice—and even managed to find him in a different prison.

Ramudu listened intently as the plan of salvation was explained through his prison bars. And he agreed to receive the printed Gospel booklet. God had begun to work in the killer's heart.

For days Ramudu read the booklet, perhaps a half-dozen times a day. The simplicity of the message touched him.

In the meantime, perhaps because of fear on the part of those who had brought charges against him, Ramudu was acquitted of the most recent murder. The criminal was once again released, and headed for home.

Back in familiar surroundings, Ramudu quickly lost interest in the Gospel. He rejoined old gang members and before long was again terrorizing small villages in the region. It was almost as if he were driven by demons.

Still, the message he had read so often in prison was now committed to memory, and seemed to haunt him in the night.

A New Creation

Not long after Ramudu returned to his village, a frail young evangelist named Samuel left the Every Home Crusade office in the same region of India to continue systematic village campaigns, conducting follow-up where other workers had visited months earlier. Where there had been multiple converts in a village with no church, Samuel sought to plant a Christ Group. One of the villages Samuel was scheduled to visit was Tumella on the Krishna River—an arduous journey of 25 miles, which he traveled by foot.

By nightfall Samuel reached the west bank of the river, but he decided not to cross it in the dark. Instead the weary evangelist found shelter in a small hut owned by an elderly woman. When she learned he was traveling to the village across the river, she warned him to be careful.

"There's a terrible murderer living there," she said haltingly. "His name is Ramudu."

Instantly God impressed on Samuel's heart that Ramudu was the reason he had come on this assignment. He had no idea two other EHC workers had already witnessed to the murderer many months earlier, while he was in prison, but he knew he had been sent to "capture" Ramudu's soul for Jesus.

Samuel looked intently at the elderly woman. "Then Ramudu is the man I must go see."

The next day at dawn, Samuel thanked his hostess and crossed the river.

Reaching the first home on the far side of the village, which the woman had identified as Ramudu's, he called out boldly, "Ramudu!"

A man with a huge head popped out the door.

"Who's there?" he shouted. Then, seeing the bag of Gospel booklets over this stranger's shoulder and apparently recognizing that he was an evangelist, he lunged toward him.

Samuel flinched, then stood in amazement as the towering Indian fell at his feet in respect. This was the customary welcome to someone new, but hardly what Samuel had expected. All he could think about, with this giant kneeling before him, was what the woman on the other side of the river had told him.

But something strange was transpiring. Ramudu stood and insisted Samuel step into his dwelling for tea.

By this time the entire village was gathering to see what was happening. Perhaps, as some suggested, Ramudu intended to murder the frail evangelist, and this was his way of mocking the man before the kill.

But Samuel stayed with Ramudu all day, listening to him and teaching him the truth of the Gospel. The seed first planted in Ramudu's heart months earlier in a prison cell was now taking root. By nightfall the apostle Paul's words would once again ring true: "If anyone is in Christ, he is a new creation" (2 Corinthians 5:17).

Frozen with Fear

Over the next 45 days Samuel continued his follow-up assignments in neighboring villages but came back repeatedly to see Ramudu.

"You must attend a church," the evangelist advised him on his fifth visit to Ramudu's home.

"But will they accept me?"

"I'll talk to the pastor of the church in the next village," the evangelist responded. "I am sure they will welcome you."

The elderly pastor expressed skepticism but agreed to look for Ramudu the following Sunday.

Meanwhile, Ramudu felt excited about going to church for the very first time. He got up early, washed and put on his best clothes. After a two-hour walk to the neighboring village, he stepped into the sanctuary.

Word had spread that Ramudu might be coming. Now the entire congregation, the men sitting on one side and the women on the other (a tradition in some Indian churches), turned to stare. The silence was deadly.

Ramudu, embarrassed, did not know what to do. Neither did the congregation. Then several fearful women stood and slipped out the side door. In moments all the remaining women followed. Almost as quickly the men's section emptied. The only person remaining in the church was the elderly pastor standing behind the pulpit. Ramudu walked boldly up to him.

The pastor froze with fear.

"I trembled as Ramudu was coming," he testified later. "Everyone knew this man was a murderer. Even the authorities feared him. I didn't know what he was going to do."

Ramudu explained why he had come. He wanted to share his testimony, he said, and become a member of the church. Then the pastor realized Ramudu had indeed become a new creature in Christ.

Soon the congregation, watching and listening from outside the building, returned one by one to the sanctuary. That very morning Ramudu gave his testimony. And within a few months he had become a familiar face among the worshipers.

Not long afterward he asked to be baptized in water. He also asked that his name be changed. He had heard the New Testament story of Saul of Tarsus who became Paul the apostle following a dramatic conversion. He had learned that Paul had murdered Christians before he found Christ and had been in prison.

So as Ramudu came up from the waters of baptism in a stream near his village, his face lit up with a glorious smile.

"From today," he exclaimed, "I shall be Paul!"

Since his dramatic conversion, Ramudu (or Paul) has been a featured speaker in many of EHC's follow-up meetings called Seekers Conferences. He has been especially helpful in nurturing ex-offenders who have come to know Jesus Christ.

And it all began with a cell-to-cell campaign to a prison. Someone with "beautiful feet" had gone where an untouchable lived—someone who might never have been touched through conventional strategies of evangelism.

Touching the Untouched

In order to reach every person with the Good News of Jesus, we must make special plans for those who fall outside the reach of normal methods of evangelism.

Ever since Jack McAlister's vision for reaching "all families of the earth" (Genesis 12:3, KJV), which we looked at earlier, Every Home for Christ has worked to take a clear presentation of the Gospel of Jesus Christ to every home. But early on it became clear that not everyone lives in what might be considered a conventional home.

Some of the untouched, like Ramudu, occupy prison cells for a significant season of their lives. Others, like university and college students, live away from home for as long as four to six years while preparing for a career, and might be missed with a conventional house-to-house strategy. Others stay in hospital settings for prolonged periods, sometimes years—captive, in a sense, to a hospital bed. And there is an entire class of world citizens who travel the seas, living for months at a time on oceangoing vessels. The only time they see land is when the ship comes into port and they enjoy a few days of shore leave.

All these are untouchables when it comes to receiving a clear presentation of the Gospel. If a strategic plan of systematic (even "saturation") evangelism calls for reaching everyone, literally, with the Gospel by taking the Good News right where they live, a plan must be developed to take the message of salvation to each of these untouchable groups as well.

In the very first house-to-house Gospel initiative conducted by Every Home for Christ in Japan in 1953, an unusual conversion amplified this need. A Christian leader planning a citywide campaign suggested, almost as an afterthought, that every cell of the prison at Fukuoka, Japan, be visited and a printed Gospel message given to each inmate. Several pastors agreed, and the prison was included in the prayer-covered campaign.

Only one inmate out of hundreds of cells visited responded—a man named Uchida. But in the months after his conversion, Uchida led more than one hundred fellow inmates to Christ. Following his own water baptism within the walls of Fukuoka prison, he sought and obtained permission to baptize any converts who agreed. At least forty did, and they formed a small Christian fellowship.

The fruit that resulted from that one "seed" planted in a cell at Fukuoka prison made it crystal clear: the Every Home Crusade needed an Every Cell Crusade. True, radio or television might reach a small percentage of inmates in a few countries. But the means to receive such mass communication are still almost nonexistent in most prison cells in the world, especially in developing countries. And although some noteworthy prison ministries, like Prison Fellowship, have had significant global impact, many of the world's incarcerated will not be touched with the Gospel unless a massive effort is mounted to go to each inmate right where he or she lives—in his or her prison cell.

Barley Paste and Pain

The ultimate goal of evangelistic house-to-house ministry—whether to conventional homes, hospital rooms, university dormitories, berths on a ship or the cells of a prison—is to bring people from darkness into light.

People like Kwonshik Lee of Korea. Kwonshik remembers when a guard at the infamous prison in Inchon, Korea, gave him his new name: Number 733. His head was shaved so guards and prison staff would know he was a prisoner, not one of them. As the barred cell door clanged shut behind him, Kwonshik, age 24, had plenty of time to reflect on his past.

He had been born into a destitute family that rarely had enough food for three meals a day. More often than not they ate simple barley paste. Many days young Kwonshik had to walk the streets, begging for food.

He had only one vague memory of those who called themselves Christians. When he was very young, he was invited to a Christmas party sponsored by a nearby church in Uwidong. He could still recall the vast array of food, and how all the poor children of the village had been invited. It was his first time hearing names like *God*, *Christ* or *Son of God*. But the real reason he had gone was the food. It was the only time he could remember in all those years that his stomach actually felt full.

But his youthful soul remained empty.

Those were days of great political turmoil. Communism was sweeping throughout the north region of Korea, including his village of Uwidong. Eventually the country would be divided. Once the Korean War was in full swing, Kwonshik fled with his family from the North, ending up in an impoverished refugee camp not far from today's Demilitarized Zone. Even the children had to fend for themselves. Then his family split up. Kwonshik was barely a teenager, filled with bitterness, hatred and loneliness.

He began searching for a job to support himself and was finally hired as a janitor at a roadside restaurant. He worked hard and befriended many prostitutes who frequented the area. Eventually Kwonshik fell into sin. But something stirred his heart with remorse. One night he remembered a few of the ideas he had heard at the Christmas party years earlier, particularly that God loved him.

But could there possibly be a God? he wondered. *If so, why is He treating me so cruelly?*

The roadside restaurant went bankrupt and Kwonshik was fired. A few weeks later he was hired by a former patron of the restaurant who needed a cook in her own rice shop. The young man worked hard for several weeks but was fired again, ostensibly for being young and inexperienced. Rage filled his heart. And when he returned a few days later to receive his final week's salary, he was told he would not be paid, that his work had not been satisfactory.

"You should be grateful you even had something to eat while working here," the shop owner shouted.

Then it happened. Kwonshik lifted a broken beer bottle with one hand and grabbed a sharp kitchen knife with the other. In moments he was looking down at a lifeless body lying in a pool of blood. He had killed the shop owner, a crime for which he was sentenced to death.

So as the door to Kwonshik's prison cell slammed behind him, he cursed God and his parents. He cursed his fellow human beings, his culture, even the country in which he had been born.

Sometime later he was transferred to the prison in Suwon, Korea, where his death sentence was to be carried out.

Then one day he spotted two young men about his age walking the corridors between the rows of prison cells, speaking to inmates and giving them booklets. Soon Kwonshik held one of the booklets in his hand. It was titled *Freedom behind Prison Bars*. It told him about a Person named Jesus Christ who could completely change his life, and it promised him something called eternal life. Anyone believing in Jesus, the booklet claimed, could experience total freedom—even if he or she had to live a lifetime behind prison bars.

The young man was fascinated with the message but uncertain about the concept of "receiving Christ as Savior." So he wrote the Korean Every Home for Christ office for more information. Then, in response to what they sent, he began working his way through the four-part EHC Bible correspondence course. He studied the first lesson and sent in the answers, but was still unsure what it all meant. In Kwonshik's words:

> In the cold and lonesome prison cell I began to study about God, the Bible, sin and Jesus Christ. What a new world there was before me! After studying the second lesson, I accepted Jesus as my personal Savior. I couldn't believe that someone would die for a murderer like me. I was totally transformed.

By the time inmate number 733 finished the Bible correspondence course, he had become a new person. The guards could tell. So could the warden. And some time later, without explanation, the government commuted Kwonshik's death sentence and pardoned him.

He never knew whether it had been a bureaucratic mistake or whether word of his behavior had touched key officials. In any case, shortly after his pardon, Kwonshik wrote this testimony:

> It has already been four years since I was put in prison. But these four years have been the most valuable and meaningful period in my life. When I first found myself behind the

clanging prison bars, I was categorized as a Class-A suspected murderer. It was a terrible label to bear. It seems as if those fearful and rebellious days in Inchon prison were only yesterday—but it was four years ago. Then I was transferred to the Suwon prison to await execution. But today I am free because someone came to my cell to tell me about Jesus. Thank God they did not miss me!

Destined for the Gallows

Years ago Every Home for Christ founder Jack McAlister stood before 1,201 inmates of another notorious Korean prison, not far from where Kwonshik Lee had been incarcerated. Jack had flown more than six thousand miles from America to observe as well as participate in this amazing commencement ceremony.

As he prepared to give each inmate a graduation certificate acknowledging his completion of the simple, four-part Bible course, Jack could not hold back the tears. Hundreds of inmates sat crowded together on a cold cement floor, their faces filled with joy, and began to sing a song they had learned only recently, "There Is Power in the Blood."

Afterward the Buddhist warden of the prison, Commandant Lee, stood and declared, "Never in all my life have I seen so many men studying the Bible and learning about Jesus Christ."

These men had given their hearts to Jesus in response to a cell-by-cell campaign to provide every inmate a salvation message. Jack calculated that it had cost less than a penny each to present all 6,540 inmates at the prison with the Gospel, resulting in the 1,201 decisions for Christ.

Little could Jack have known that in the following several decades, more than six million inmates would be visited, cell by cell, and more than 120,000 inmates would complete a similar Bible course and pray to receive Jesus as Savior.

Are these conversions genuine? An answer can be found in the testimony of one of the 1,201 inmates Jack met during the ceremony in Korea.

Indoh Park, a colonel from the North Korean army and a political prisoner condemned to death, was the first man to receive his diploma at the mass prison graduation. Earlier, after his conversion through a printed Gospel message given to him in his cell, Colonel Park had written the EHC office in Korea:

> All my life I have been afraid of what will happen after death. Even in the fiercest battle during the war in the North, this matter bewildered me. But now, after accepting Christ as my personal Savior, my death sentence does not make me afraid. I can confess that I am truly happy. I will continue to study the Bible lessons until I lay down my life and go to be with Jesus.

When Jack McAlister left the prison, he embraced Colonel Park and encouraged him to be strong in the Lord. The condemned inmate smiled and responded, "Christ is nearer to me than ever before."

Colonel Park probably sensed what lay immediately ahead. His final appeal to the Supreme Court of South Korea was denied, and a few weeks later he was hanged. But those who knew him had little doubt Colonel Park was a new creation in Christ.

Perhaps of the 1,201 prisoners who found Christ at that Korean prison, there is special significance in the very last digit of that number. There was *one* named Colonel Indoh Park, and today he is with Jesus.

10
Warriors of the Night

Nights seem darker in China, and this night was no exception. Perhaps it was the absence of street lights, I thought. Or perhaps it was the spiritual darkness that seemed to hover over this section of high-rise apartments on the outskirts of one of China's large northern cities.

It was past midnight, and the team of night warriors I was working with had already distributed almost a thousand Gospel messages. Our small team of four had split up into two groups. Another group of four had gone to a different area of the city. For several hours we had been darting in and out of shadowy entrances to apartment buildings, keeping our eyes open for the authorities or anyone who might detect what we were doing. Cars, although common these days in China, were scarce at that time of night, and any time we caught the glare of headlights, we knew they were from either a taxi or a police car. Discovery by either could lead to serious consequences.

Suddenly we heard someone coming through the entryway of one of the apartments where we had just distributed scores of Gospel messages. We darted once again into the shadows. My heart pounded as we stood in absolute silence. But it was a false alarm. No doubt the person thought he had heard something, and then walked back quietly into his apartment.

I took a deep breath and thought to myself again, *I can't believe I'm here in the middle of northern China breaking the law! What on earth ever came over me to agree to do this?*

For years I had had a special burden for China and had prayed for that nation every day I could remember for more than nineteen years.

Every Home for Christ also took the call to prayer very seriously. Two decades earlier the ministry had printed thirty separate pamphlets for prayer, each focusing on a different province of China. We were also involved with various Christian organizations and indigenous church groups to get Bibles and other Christian literature into China. As far back as the early 1960s, we had filled balloons with Gospel booklets and released them with favorable winds from Taiwan into the coastal areas of southern China. It was the best we could do at the time, and a modest but encouraging number of mailed responses indicated fruit. Still, the doors seemed to be closed tightly to any kind of systematic activity to take the Gospel home to home in China.

Now here I was, in June 1995, with a small team of Western Christians in the middle of the night, going from apartment to apartment, sharing the Good News of Jesus Christ and hoping we would not get caught.

We were part of an emerging strategy that fascinated me— one that I had heard about only recently, and which had been implemented for little more than sixteen months throughout China. It had all been started (as I was to discover) by a passionate 21-year-old British lad with only a ninth-grade education and a call from God to forsake everything and go to China.

Meeting Brother Fu

My unusual experience with these "warriors of the night" began five months earlier, when ten EHC national directors from East and Southeast Asia gathered in January 1995 in Hong Kong to strategize for the remaining years of the decade. China was high on our list of priorities. But the big question concerned the feasibility of conducting systematic, home-by-home evangelism there. We had heard many remarkable reports coming out of that vast land, some indicating as many as 35,000 conversions a day. But all forms of open evangelism were outlawed, even though we knew that if a systematic plan ever were permitted the numbers would be far higher. Most of us at the meeting agreed that a systematic plan to evangelize China simply could not be implemented, at least for now.

Then I met a young British brother whom I will call, for security reasons, Brother Fu.[1]

I might not have met Brother Fu had it not been for an unexpected encounter with a respected missionary who works in China. I talked with him only moments after my arrival in East Asia for the EHC leaders' conference. Exhausted from more than 24 hours of nonstop travel, I was ready to fall into bed when the phone rang.

The missionary, with whom I had hoped to meet while I was in the area, was calling to inform me he was leaving for the United States early the next morning. If I wanted to touch base with him, it had to be that night.

Something within me—I know now it was God's Spirit—urged me to see him in spite of my exhaustion. So moments later we were seated in the hotel lobby as he related to me incredible stories of what was happening in China.

Suddenly, almost midsentence, he looked me in the eyes and asked, "So, Dick, what are your plans for China?"

I explained the vision of Every Home for Christ and how our ultimate goal was to work with believers in China, as we have done in more than 190 other countries, to take a printed message of salvation to literally every family.

I was startled when the missionary interrupted me.

"I think that's already begun," he said. "There's a British chap here, only in his twenties, who's doing an amazing work just as you're describing. You really need to see him."

"Is that possible?" I asked excitedly.

"Yes. He just arrived today from Beijing and will be here through the weekend. It's great you came this week," he added. "This brother shows up here only a few days every other month. The rest of the time he's running all over China."

As I tumbled into bed an hour or two later, I knew in my heart that God had been setting up circumstances for a strategic encounter that would change my thinking about the evangelization of China.

Less than 36 hours later I met Brother Fu. His wrinkled blue sport coat fit tightly on his thin frame, and his narrow, old-fashioned tie clashed with his shirt. But style, I soon realized, mattered little to Brother Fu. He cared only about souls. And he had left his home in Great Britain because Chinese people by the millions needed to hear about Jesus.

Only a few days after first meeting Brother Fu, and after a night of prayer, God impressed a thought on my heart: *You can never know the joy of giving people the Gospel in a restricted nation until you've experienced it for yourself.*

So it was that I found myself, five months later, joined to a team of Western warriors of the night, distributing Gospel literature in one of the closed nations of the world.

A New Home

In some ways, Fu is about as ordinary as you get. Some might even say he is less than ordinary. As a seventeen-year-old, he left school after the ninth grade and volunteered to work for free on a pig farm near his home while the owners went on vacation. He worked so hard they kept him on after they returned. Later Fu's parents, pleased with his determination to make a way for himself, gave him a hundred acres of farmland to help him get started in life with his own small farm.

Fu was destined to be a farmer, it seemed, reaping a harvest of sorghum and beans. But God had another kind of harvest for him. Someone shared the Good News of Jesus with him and his life was transformed. He knew, though he was still in his teens, that God had a plan for his life. If that meant sorghum and beans for Jesus, then sorghum and beans for Jesus it would be.

But Fu was stirred in his heart about the possibility of full-time Christian ministry. He knew he lacked a good education, but he also knew God could help him make up for it.

Then in 1987 a small team of Christians came to Fu's little church in central England to recount their experiences taking Bibles into China. When they said they planned another trip into China just four months later, Fu was instantly convinced this was what he should do. He just knew.

"I honestly didn't even pray about it," he told me as we talked. "I just told everybody, 'I'm going to China.' To be honest, it sounded like fun."

Four months later he accompanied that team to one of East Asia's key cities, where they were briefed on how to take Bibles inconspicuously into China. They would not deliver their Bibles immediately to Chinese contacts, but wait several days while they saw the sights like all tourists. Then they would meet some local believers—they were given specific instructions as to where and how—and give their precious "bread" to them.

As Fu cleared customs with a backpack and other luggage filled with Bibles, he heard a still, small voice speaking to his heart: *You've arrived at your new home.*

This message, which had flooded his heart in an instant, would change his life.

"I just knew I was home," Fu told me. "From then on there was no question about where I was to live."

The more he saw of the Chinese people, the more his heart was broken. There were so many in China who had no understanding of salvation through Christ. He would lie awake at night wondering, *How can we get the Word to them? How can we give them the Good News?*

While traveling to Beijing on that first trip, something happened to Brother Fu that would influence the direction of his mission for China.

Having given the bulk of his Chinese Bibles to his contact, Fu wondered how he might best use his remaining Bibles. They were just a few compared to the vast multitudes in Beijing. Trusting the Holy Spirit to guide him, he walked casually to a busy street corner. When it appeared that no one was watching, he placed a Bible on a ledge near a lamppost, then darted quickly into the shadows. The very first person who spotted the Bible snatched it up as though he were seizing priceless treasure.

So Fu sauntered back to the spot and, after a few moments, dropped another Bible. It, too, was grabbed up.

After repeating the process several times in several locations, the young Brit realized that even if he could continue this pace of distributing God's Word in China indefinitely, it would take centuries to make a dent in the vast spiritual need of the Chinese people. On the one hand, he felt encouraged that a few seeds had been planted. But he was troubled at the seeming impossibility of the task of getting the Gospel to the millions of Chinese.

When Fu's short visa expired, he had no choice but to return to his homeland—in spite of the impression from God that his new home was really China. But within three months he had sold all his possessions and, in January 1988, returned once again to China.

In Beijing, through a Chinese Christian he had met earlier, he approached several universities and offered them his services as an English teacher, although he realized he lacked the educational qualifications for a teaching job. Sure enough, the moment they heard he had only a ninth-grade education, they declined. Fu became increasingly discouraged and soon began questioning the Lord. Had God really told him China would be his new home?

Then in prayer he became convinced he had been operating in his own strength, rather than in God's strength, and decided to turn the matter over to the Lord. Only God could get a twenty-year-old with a ninth-grade education a job as an English teacher in China!

The following Sunday Fu was invited to visit a small gathering of Christian students in Beijing. Following a Bible study, several of the students were chatting about spiritual things. Then one of the female students addressed Fu.

"I understand you are looking for a job teaching English?"

Fu was stunned. How had she known?

"Yes, I am," he replied.

"Well, I'm teaching English in a hotel, and they're looking for other teachers."

She named the number-one hotel in all of China for foreigners at the time, and agreed to set up an interview.

Within days Fu was teaching English to excited Chinese students who wanted desperately to learn the language. They had no idea their instructor was staying up late into the night trying to figure out the difference between verbs and adverbs!

The job lasted a full year—just enough time for Fu to establish a base and to learn the Chinese language for himself. Also during that time, God began to show the young man His plan for communicating the Gospel systematically, through the printed page, to every family across China. Fittingly, it all began in Beijing, China's capital city.

Brother Fu noticed quickly that Beijing's city center, the original part of the city, consisted of lanes—very narrow streets with small individual dwellings along either side. This was a holdover from the British influence more than a half-century earlier. Most of the newer, outer parts of the city consisted of huge, multifamily high-rises (typical in Communist-ruled countries). All those high-rises, as Brother Fu was quick to note, had mailboxes (or, as the British would say, *letterboxes*) that would make it easier to reach every family.

A plan was emerging in Brother Fu's mind. He recalled how readily people snatched up the few Bibles he had put onto ledges near street corners just a few months earlier. Because he had done this discreetly and no one had seen him, he knew he had not been reported to authorities. What if he dressed Chinese and went out at night on his bicycle distributing Gospel messages? Wouldn't it be possible to reach hundreds of families a night and have no one be any the wiser?

Trouble in Tiananmen Square

During those days, as the vision grew in Fu's heart, a devastating event occurred in China that affected him deeply. In fact, he found himself strangely caught up in the middle of it.

Fu had just turned 21 and had been in China only a year and a half. For reasons no one fully understood, huge throngs of university students were flocking to Beijing's famous Tiananmen Square. They brought with them a unified call for democratic reforms. Everyone was filled with excitement. No one seemed to sense the turmoil that lay ahead.

On June 3, 1989, Fu went to see an eighty-year-old Chinese woman we will call Mildred, who often served as a stopping-off point for Gospel literature that had come into China from outside sources. Mildred told Fu she had just received a shipment of more Gospel messages. Did he want them? Fu had exhausted nearly all of his supply and was delighted to accept a large tote bag half-full of unfolded Gospel messages. It easily contained three thousand tracts. Fu could not wait to distribute them.

Shortly before midnight, as he was riding his bicycle back to his hotel, he passed Tiananmen Square. Thousands of young people were still gathering, and hundreds of tents had been erected. Then he thought of his tote bag, and a strange burden flooded his heart, accompanied by a sense of urgency.

He was dressed in his usual Chinese garb—a dark blue Mao jacket with dark pants and a typical Chinese hat with its long bill. He knew he would be inconspicuous. So he pulled the bill of his cap down over his forehead and pedaled toward the center of the square.

Then Fu did something unusual. He stopped his bicycle and stood quietly, lifting his face toward heaven. In Jesus' name he claimed authority over the forces of darkness, binding them as Jesus instructed His disciples in Matthew 16:19: "Whatever you bind on earth will be bound in heaven, and whatever you loose on earth will be loosed in heaven." Then Fu claimed souls that night for Jesus. It was exactly midnight.

Clutching his tote bag tightly, Fu began to walk among the hundreds of tents set up in the square. When no one was looking, he threw a handful of messages into a tent. If he could hear students in the tent talking, he lay a small stack of messages by the entrance and walked hastily on.

Scores of tents were served with the Gospel in those late-night hours. Fu nearly emptied his bag. Then he prayed, *Let them read the message tonight, Lord. Open their eyes to Your plan of salvation.*

Less than 24 hours later, hundreds of these very students would lie lifeless in pools of blood, their bodies scattered across the massive square.

Late that night, back at his hotel, Fu heard gunfire. And the following morning, when he rode his bicycle back to Tiananmen Square, he discovered carnage in all directions, and buses everywhere turned upside down and burning. The crackdown on the pro-democracy movement had started.

Suddenly one of the soldiers fired tear gas and everyone scattered. Fu pedaled to the other side of the square, opposite the famed Hall of the People. When the soldiers were not looking, he took out his camera and began taking pictures. Instantly and without warning, a row of soldiers began opening fire in different directions. People were screaming and running, and Fu took off like a rocket. He knew he was in a war zone.

At the hotel, Fu was told that all foreigners had to report to the airport immediately. And soon he found himself once again on his way back to his homeland. His China call would be interrupted for several months. But as soon as he was able, Fu returned to China—this time, Lord willing, for good.

Bicycle Baskets and Doorsteps

Fu's experience at Tiananmen Square convinced him he had to do all he could to get the Gospel to every Chinese person possible. He knew he had to do it even if other respected mission leaders criticized this method, saying it endangered local Chinese Christians. Soon he was riding his bicycle late at night, every few nights, up and down the lanes of central Beijing. He tossed Gospel messages, when no one was looking, into bicycle baskets and onto doorsteps. Dropping a tract into a bicycle basket, Fu knew, was the same as leaving it in their home, since it seemed everyone in China had a bicycle.

During his first year Fu visited some ten thousand homes, always trying to keep a record of where he had been so he would not cover an area twice, especially when so many parts of the city had not been reached once. At first Fu still taught English during the day, while at night he put on his Chinese garb and went out with the Gospel.

"My greatest hindrance," Fu told me, "wasn't the lack of sleep, but the lack of literature. Sometimes I had to wait many weeks before another team came from the outside with a fresh supply of Gospel messages."

After the Tiananmen Square massacre, the work accelerated dramatically. Until then Fu had told no one about his activities, not even missionary friends. He felt it was too risky.

Then one day a fresh team of couriers, led by his friend John, came from the West with Bibles. He met them at the border and agreed to help them make contact with Chinese believers. But first they had to wait three days. Fu suggested to John that perhaps there were some tourist sights they might see.

"Look," said John, "I didn't come to see sights but to save souls. Isn't there something we can do to help get people the Gospel?"

Fu decided to tell his friend what he had been doing, and invited him to try it a night or two. John accepted with joy, and they decided to invite the others on the team to join them.

So successful was the outreach that they planned several more night campaigns. John and his team would return to their country and invite other courageous believers to join them. Soon a plan was underway to help the teams move out into many additional Chinese communities.

As Fu began to research the towns and cities of China, he discovered there were at least 574 cities with a population of between three and four thousand. (Other much larger cities, like Beijing and Shanghai, have populations in the millions.) Within the next 24 months, Fu would visit two hundred of these cities personally, planting Gospel seeds in each one but also gathering maps of the various locales to prepare for systematic tract-planting outreaches. Then the young strategist compiled this information in small, printed "tourist guides" for each province to be targeted (information that proved an invaluable aid to the team of night warriors I joined in June 1995).

Fu also realized that many of the larger cities, at least five hundred of them, could serve as bases from which teams could travel to smaller towns at night and share the Good News. They could come into a city during the day, and late that night share printed Gospel messages throughout an assigned area of the city. By the next morning, usually before dawn, they could catch one of the typical Chinese minibuses and leave town, even as the residents of that city were waking up to discover life-giving salvation messages in their bicycle baskets or mailboxes or even on their doorsteps.

There was yet another dimension to Fu's literature distribution ministry that fascinated me, facilitated by those Chinese minibuses, which carried 15 to 25 passengers each to towns throughout China. He called it "tract-bombing." It was also the most controversial dimension.

In one of his early trips to a distant town, a trip that took at least five hours, Fu decided to sit in the rear of the bus by a window. Beside him was his bag loaded with Gospel booklets for distribution in the town where he was heading. As the bus rumbled through small villages, rarely slowing down even for pedestrians, an idea came to him. Fu decided, when no one was looking, to toss a handful of booklets out the window.

The result was amazing. The wind hit the booklets and scattered them across the road like a white carpet of paper, while people came running from all directions to retrieve one of them. Some even stood in the middle of the road as they read the Gospel message.

Other teams eventually came to participate, and tract-bombing became an exciting part of the evangelistic experience. Only later would I learn how controversial it was to some missionary leaders. They claimed that it put local Chinese Christians in danger of being blamed for doing it. But then I heard of amazing testimonies of the fruit of such a strategy, including almost a whole village in one province coming to Christ and a church being started in that village as the result of a farmer picking up a tract by the side of a road as a bus passed by.

I subsequently heard that many local believers were glad outsiders had come to do this, no matter the risks. Some even said they were so moved by the courage of these Westerners that they decided that they needed to do this, too.

So, I'm glad I experienced it firsthand—including the delight of tossing more than two thousand Gospel booklets in small "cluster bombs" out a minibus window into the Chinese countryside. One cluster scattered near a group of schoolchildren, who came running from everywhere. As the bus rumbled on, I turned and watched as one girl, probably not more than ten years old, stood in the middle of the road reading the message intently. I felt the Holy Spirit speak in my heart, "That's the first time she has ever heard that Jesus Christ loves her."

By the time my team's two-week mission was completed, more than two hundred thousand Gospel messages had been planted within hand's reach of waiting Chinese people.

Conflicting Commandments

One of the great challenges in attempting to evangelize a nation considered closed to the Gospel is how to reconcile the Scripture passages that on the one hand command believers *everywhere* to take the Good News to *everybody*, and on the other hand admonish followers of Jesus to obey those in authority.

But then we recall how the disciples in Acts 5:17–29 were told by the ruling authorities to cease all teaching about Jesus. Up to that point they had been going freely throughout Jerusalem and seeing significant results as multitudes turned to the Lord. But, we read, "The high priest and all his associates, who were members of the party of the Sadducees, were filled with jealousy" (verse 17). They had the apostles arrested and jailed.

It was another opportunity for a miracle, as an angel appeared to them at night and released them. He told them, "Go, stand in the temple courts . . . and tell the people the full message of this new life" (verse 20).

The disciples obeyed, and on the very day of their release were again spotted in the Temple teaching people about Jesus. Again they were arrested and brought before the high priest for questioning.

> "We gave you strict orders not to teach in this name," he said.
> "Yet you have filled Jerusalem with your teaching."
>
> Acts 5:28

Quite simply, the apostles had been breaking the law. But Peter and the others replied, "We must obey God rather than men!" (verse 29).

Through the intervention of Gamaliel, a respected teacher of the law, they were released, but not before being beaten and ordered once again not to speak about Jesus.

But we read only two verses later not only that they continued to testify about Jesus, but that they did it "day after day, in the temple courts and from house to house" (verse 42). That verse adds, in fact: "They never stopped teaching and proclaiming the good news that Jesus is the Christ."

In contrast to the disciples' clear violation of the law, what do we make of Paul's equally inspired directive in Romans?

> Everyone must submit himself to the governing authorities, for there is no authority except that which God has established. The authorities that exist have been established by God. . . . Therefore, it is necessary to submit to the authorities, not only because of possible punishment but also because of conscience.
>
> Romans 13:1, 5

Certainly engaging in strictly prohibited evangelism is in direct opposition to the governing authorities of a nation. We must recognize, however, that we have a mandate from the Lord to take the Good News to literally every person (see again Matthew 28:19 and Mark 16:15). The conduct of the apostles shows us that whenever man-made laws contradict the clear teaching of God's Word, the believer is duty-bound to submit to God first. This is exactly what Brother Fu felt about his work in China.

Numerous examples in Scripture (in addition to the Acts 5 examples above) illustrate this principle. Here are three:

1. *The midwives* refused to obey Pharaoh's order to kill all male babies born to the Hebrew women in Egypt (see Exodus 1:15–21). God rewarded those midwives for what they did.
2. *Shadrach, Meshach and Abednego* refused to worship the idol the Babylonian king had set up and found themselves thrown into the fiery furnace (see Daniel 3). God delivered them and even caused them to be promoted by the king.
3. *Daniel* continued to pray to his God in defiance of King Darius's decree forbidding prayer to any god except the king himself (see Daniel 6). God "sent his angel, and he shut the mouths of the lions" (verse 22) after Daniel was punished for breaking the law. God not only kept Daniel from certain death, but actually prospered him during the reigns of Darius and Cyrus.

So I felt comfortable, biblically speaking, darting up and down those darkened alleyways (even though it did not lessen my anxieties of the moment!). We were breaking Chinese law, but I also knew we were obeying the commission Christ gave the Church to go into all the world and preach the Good News to everybody. Furthermore, I had the distinct sense that if we were caught, we could trust God to deliver us in His own way, just as He did Daniel and the early disciples.

A Minibus Miracle

Best of all, we saw firsthand evidence that God was honoring the planting of these seeds. One unique testimony came to our attention the very last day of our June 1995 evangelism adventure.

As we gathered for a final debriefing, two of the brothers on the team, who had journeyed the farthest into the province, shared a most incredible encounter.

While they rode their minibus to a remote town, they told us, they began releasing clusters of booklets out the back window whenever the passengers seemed distracted. They were helped inadvertently in the process by a Chinese woman in her early twenties who was sitting near the front of the bus, reading to other Chinese riders from a booklet in her hand and explaining its contents.

Suddenly one of the Christian workers, a foreign brother who knew some Mandarin Chinese, turned to his partner.

"She's talking about Jesus!" he exclaimed with a stunned look on his face. "I'm sure of it!"

He listened more carefully, picking up words and phrases like *repentance* and *personal Savior*. To his amazement, he realized she was now giving an invitation to receive Christ— and several on the bus were responding!

When she had finished, one of the young workers approached the student evangelist and asked if she spoke any English. She understood enough to communicate, and told the workers she had found Christ four years earlier. When they asked her how she had come to Christ, she pulled a sixteen-page booklet from her purse that she had used in her preaching. It was actually a photocopy of a booklet.

"This booklet told me about Jesus," she explained, clutching it happily. "I found it by my door one morning four years ago."

"Is this the original booklet?" asked one of the workers.

"Oh, no," she answered quickly. "This is a copy. I've made many copies of the booklet since then, and I've given them away to people who want to meet Jesus." She then explained that many had received Christ as a result.

"Do you have an extra copy I might keep?" she was asked.

"Oh, yes, I have many extra copies."

Now, as our evangelism team sat crammed together in a Chinese hotel room for our final debriefing, one of the brothers from the team produced the booklet for the entire group to see.

In that instant I happened to be looking at Brother Fu, whose eyes filled with tears. Quickly he spoke up.

"This is one of the very booklets I planted in that same town late at night four years ago," he said, "when I first came to map the cities of this province." Then he smiled like a child who had just won a prize. "I must have left that booklet by her doorway."

I smiled, too, as I felt Brother Fu's joy. And I thought of God's promise to Isaiah: "[My word] will not return to me empty, but will accomplish what I desire and achieve the purpose for which I sent it" (Isaiah 55:11).

11
Cords of Completion

He was a man with a vision for "completion"—that elusive term missiologists and evangelism strategists use to define the ultimate fulfillment of the Great Commission. Even though his most productive years of ministry came at the end of the nineteenth century, Dr. A. T. Pierson's passionate pursuit of closure, a term he probably never actually used, is almost legendary. His heart beat for the completion of world evangelization in his lifetime and he spread this vision to all who would listen.

It was Dr. Pierson, a pastor and gifted writer with a missionary's heart, who trumpeted the cause of finishing the task of world evangelization by the year 1900. As far back as 1870, when the vision gripped his heart, Pierson was convinced it was possible.

The preaching of the great American evangelist Dwight L. Moody in England had been stirring up the Church in the British Isles. Young people especially were being touched. In early 1885 seven outstanding students from Cambridge University, soon to be known as the "Cambridge Seven," set sail for missionary service in China under the famous China Inland Mission, founded by J. Hudson Taylor.

In 1885, with a full fifteen years remaining until the turn of the century, the vision to fulfill the Great Commission was spreading. Closure actually seemed possible. At a conference in Northfield, Massachusetts, attended by a thousand key leaders and lay Christians, A. T. Pierson, accompanied by D. L. Moody, presented the vision.

Pierson preached with passion about finishing the task of global evangelization by the year 1900. His words were filled with hope. Boldly he declared,

> If 10 million out of 400 million nominal Christians would undertake such systematic labors that each one of that number should in the course of the next 15 years reach 100 other souls with the gospel message, the whole present population of the globe would have heard the Good Tidings by the year 1900![1]

It is reported that D. L. Moody leaped to his feet, interrupting Pierson and shouting to the crowd, "How many of you believe this can be done?" The crowd cheered in agreement as if to cast their unanimous vote to move ahead toward the goal. The same night Moody appointed a committee of six and agreed to participate himself in seeking God's direction to finish the task of global evangelism "now!"

In three days the small group had prepared a document entitled "An Appeal to Disciples Everywhere." It was presented to the entire delegation still in session and approved by another thunderous cheer. Included in the document was a call for a global conference of key leaders in which plans could be set forth for finishing the task.

A year later, in 1886, Dr. Pierson published a book, *Crisis in Missions*, that spelled out the incredible opportunities that lay before a stirred-up Church. "An Appeal to Disciples Everywhere" appeared in its appendix.

The Church seemed poised to finish the Great Commission Christ had given His disciples nearly nineteen centuries earlier.

Then in 1888 another world missions conference took place, this one in London. It had been in the planning stages even before the Northfield Conference. Some hoped it would set into motion strategies (as suggested by "An Appeal to Disciples Everywhere") that could be implemented to fulfill the Great Commission. Instead it emerged as an inspirational conference only, stirring up the participants' emotions but resulting in no significant world evangelism strategy.

As the millennium approached, hopes dimmed for reaching the goal. By 1895 A. T. Pierson finally declared, "We're compelled to give up the hope."[2]

The Quest for Completion

At least two factors were at work hindering the achievement of what had been a plausible goal. The question today is whether the Church will succumb once again to the same hindrances.

It is said that when Dr. Pierson and his colleagues felt "compelled to give up the hope" to evangelize the world by the year 1900, he attributed the failure to two primary areas of neglect. First, the corporate Church did not cooperate fully in the task. They talked about it and preached about it but never sat down and planned practically how they could do it together. And second, the Church did not mobilize enough prayer.

These two obstacles are far less formidable today as we move into a new millennium. In fact, there are more hopeful signs today regarding global prayer movements than at any previous time in history. At the end of the nineteenth century, what was happening regarding the mobilization of prayer could not even come close to what is taking place at present. Furthermore, an ever-increasing spirit of cooperation among missions groups, organizations, denominations and strategies is breaking down sectarianism and ministry isolationism that have slowed the Church so often in her past quests for closure.

Prayer Mobilization

First, regarding prayer mobilization, Anglican researcher David Barrett suggests there may be as many as 170 million Christians worldwide committed to praying every day for spiritual awakening and world evangelization. Of this number, he says, as many as twenty million believers actually see intercession as their primary calling and ministry within Christ's Body.[3]

There may be as many as ten million groups meeting regularly, adds Barrett, with the primary focus of praying for world revival. Equally astounding, the researcher says there may be as many as thirteen hundred separate prayer mobilization networks seeking to motivate and mobilize the Church to pray for global spiritual awakening and the evangelization of the lost.[4]

Prayer is the key to the completion of the Great Commission, as we will highlight in the final chapter.

Working Together

Something else extraordinary is happening, which we will look at in this chapter: Ministries, denominations and strategies are uniting to work together toward the common goal of fulfilling the Great Commission in our generation. According to David Bryant in his book *The Hope at Hand* (Baker Books, 1995), a global network of evangelical missions has emerged over the last 25 years, including such strategic alliances as the Lausanne Committee for World Evangelization, the A.D. 2000 & Beyond Movement, the International Charismatic Congress on World Evangelization and the World Evangelical Alliance.[5]

Bryant further points out a spontaneous networking of plans worldwide that has since emerged. As many as seventy international strategies are focused on total world evangelization as we settle into the twenty-first century. In addition, Bryant says, there are currently 56 "Great Commission global networks" uniting ministries concentrated on all the two hundred–plus nations in the world and seeking the fulfillment of the Great Commission.[6]

The Rallying Cry

Whether or not the Great Commission is completed literally in the decade or two just ahead, it is healthy to see the extraordinary way so many global evangelism strategies are coming together to cooperate toward that goal.

This became especially clear to me during a forty-day fast during March and April of the year 2000. I became convinced that the task of world evangelization could not be completed by any one group. On the contrary, it would require something of a miracle of cooperation not yet seen in the twenty-first century.

I thought of the many times I had been in prayer settings (including each morning with our staff in our office) when prayer was offered for ours and other ministries, that God would knit us all together. Often I joined in that prayer, intending to ask God to give us a "spirit of networking." But each time I tried to say the word networking, it came out "knit-working." This happened for several months.

At first it seemed like a slip of the tongue. Then I began to realize it was something the Holy Spirit was orchestrating—a new picture of cooperation. We needed to weave our strategies and ministries much more closely together, I realized, just as something knit together is woven more tightly than something that is simply strung together.

Mustering Our Joint Forces

Two passages of Scripture come to mind. First, the Old Testament account of Israel's rebellious tribe, Benjamin, in which a concubine was raped and her dead body cut into twelve parts and sent throughout all Israel. The eleven other tribes attacked the Benjamite city of Gibeah because of the crime (see Judges 20:1–11). Three times in this brief passage (verses 1, 8, 11) we are told that Israel joined together "as one man." Note especially the description from verse 11: "All the men of Israel were gathered against the city, knit together as one man" (KJV).

The Hebrew word for "knit together," *chaber*, means "to be in association with; to be united; to be a close companion in a task or cause." *Chaber* comes from a Hebrew root meaning "to join together; to partner together." Moffatt translated verse 11 this way: "They mustered their joint forces."

Each of the eleven tribes, to an extent, had its own goals and objectives. Each had its own warriors and, no doubt, its own ideas as to how the situation ought to be handled. Any of the tribes could have mobilized its individual resources in an attempt to punish the tribe of Benjamin. But instead "they mustered their joint forces" toward a common purpose. And although the final victory did not come until the third wave of attack, and then only after a season of weeping before the Lord with fasting (see Judges 20:18–26), any one of the eleven tribes attempting the task alone might well have been annihilated. Being "knit together as one" was the key.

The same is true, I am convinced, if fulfillment of the Great Commission is to be achieved in our generation.

A Fabric of Harmony

The other Scripture that comes to mind when I think about how we need to weave our strategies and ministries more closely together is Paul's "knit-working" portrayal of the Body of Christ. He described the uniting of various functions of the Church, specifically involving the use of the various apostolic gifts. These gifts, he wrote, are to help bring God's people to His overall objective:

> [To be] built up until we all reach unity in the faith and in the knowledge of the Son of God and become mature, attaining to the whole measure of the fullness of Christ.
>
> Ephesians 4:12–13

Paul went on to describe Christ's role in this process: "From him the whole body, joined and held together by every supporting ligament, grows and builds itself up in love, as each part does its work" (verse 16).

The King James Version refers to the whole body as being "fitly joined together." The Amplified Bible uses the equally accurate expression "firmly knit together." Each of these versions is translating the Greek word *sumbibazo*, a combination of the Greek *sum*, a prime root meaning "union with" or "together," and *bibazo*, meaning "to force" or "to drive." *Sumbibazo* is thus speaking of something that is driven together or even forced together for a purpose.

When we first started getting together with various consultations in the 1990s to consider ways to cooperate toward completing the Great Commission, God had already begun a process of *sumbibazo* throughout Christ's Body, especially regarding ministries with a focus on world evangelization. He was driving us together for a purpose. Indeed, in some ways it even seemed we were being forced together.

For one thing, most missions (including the participants in our consultation) were facing declining resources, even as opportunities for expansion were increasing dramatically. For another thing, not only the old Soviet Union but all of Eastern Europe was open to evangelistic activity for the first time in seven decades. China, too, was becoming more open. Also, it was becoming increasingly obvious that there were still significant enemy strongholds blocking the path toward completion—countries like the Arab-Muslim nations that still blocked public or open evangelization.

All these factors can easily hinder any one strategy or group from achieving its objectives. But by mustering their joint forces, these groups might overcome all such challenges. Could it be the Lord is compelling His Church to come together? Is the Lord of the harvest weaving His "cords of completion" on a loom of adversity and opportunity because He knows this is the only way His people will work together to complete the task?

Networking is essential, of course, but in a spirit of greater closeness, which we might think of more as *knit-working*. Knit-working is what you and I do to weave our lives and ministries with others in such a way that we create a beautiful fabric of harmony. And when it comes to world evangelization, this fabric will help cover all the earth with the Good News of Christ's love.

12
The Fate of the World

Writing in his classic book *Destined for the Throne*, Dr. Paul E. Billheimer reminds us that "the fate of the world is in the hands of nameless saints."[1] Billheimer was speaking of the unseen servants and soldiers in the battle for men's souls who give, go and pray but rarely get the credit. Billheimer's quote always reminds me of F. C. Case, a quiet woodcutter who lived his entire life in the same North Carolina cabin where he was born.

F. C. Case was not a man of great means. In fact, even when he was well past seventy, he still read by the light of a kerosene lantern. Only a few years before his death at age 86 did Frank finally bring electricity into his cabin—and that was mainly because it took so many batteries to power his radio (which he kept tuned to Christian programming)!

The old man's diet often consisted of little more than a ten-dollar bag of pinto beans, which he said might last him almost a month. His sole income in his later years came from cutting and chopping wood in the Carolina hills (although he never owned anything as modern as a chain saw) and selling it in nearby towns. Yet this man was responsible for providing printed Gospel messages for more than eight million people in scores of countries around the world.

F. C. Case entered life, as he put it, "a full-blooded Baptist," and he joined his church officially at age sixteen. Shortly after becoming a Christian, Frank began giving to missions. He tithed faithfully to his church and often doubled and tripled that amount to missions.

During the Depression Frank earned as little as fifty cents a day working on bridge construction, even less when he made bricks or sold wood. Because fifteen people were eating from his table, he had to stretch a bag of pinto beans for up to two months—though he was never quite sure how he did it! But he never wavered from his commitment to give to missions. By the end of the Depression, he was giving ten dollars a month to missions—a remarkable sum when you consider that it was equivalent to the price of two months of food.

Early in the 1950s, at a church missions convention, the Lord spoke to F. C. Case about giving a thousand dollars to buy literature for India. Until then he had never heard about the impact of literature in evangelism. Now he felt God leading him to give a huge sum for this purpose. A few weeks later Frank heard Jack McAlister over the radio talking about conducting Every Home Crusades throughout the world, using Gospel literature. Frank sent an initial gift of two dollars. He considered it a small down payment toward his overall goal.

Through the years Frank's gifts grew remarkably. It often seemed he was giving everything he had except the few dollars he needed to eat. In many months Frank sent as much as six hundred dollars, earned from cutting wood in the North Carolina hills. And always he covered his gifts with prayer.

When Frank Case heard about how inexpensive and effective systematic literature evangelism is, he was inspired to do much more. He calculated how many people he could reach with a dollar (at that time, one hundred families could be reached!), and he set a personal goal of reaching ten million people with the Gospel in his lifetime.

When F. C. Case died in 1976, he was two million short of reaching his goal. But he knew that eight million people had been given access to the Gospel because of his faithfulness.

Not Many Noble

The self-giving life of F. C. Case reminds me of the apostle Paul's words:

> Brothers, think of what you were when you were called. Not many of you were wise by human standards; not many were influential; not many were of noble birth.
>
> 1 Corinthians 1:26

These words of Paul's, coupled with Paul Billheimer's wise insight, remind us that it really is a host of "nameless saints" like F. C. Case who will make possible the ultimate fulfillment of the Great Commission.

When Paul spoke to the believers at Rome about what was necessary for spreading the Gospel everywhere, he made a sweeping declaration: "Everyone who calls on the name of the Lord will be saved" (Romans 10:13). Then the apostle asked a series of questions:

> How . . . can they call on the one they have not believed in? And how can they believe in the one of whom they have not heard? And how can they hear without someone preaching to them?
>
> verse 14

Finally Paul asked the pivotal question: "And how can they preach unless they are sent?" (verse 15). The apostle added quickly, quoting the prophet Isaiah, "How beautiful are the feet of those who bring good news!" (see Isaiah 52:7).

Paul was speaking of those behind-the-scenes senders without whom the fulfillment of the Great Commission would remain a dream. They are the givers and pray-ers, the nameless saints who, in Jesus, control the destiny of human beings and nations.

And at the heart of their calling is the ministry of prayer.

Change the World

From the moment Jack McAlister knelt prayerfully with Ken McVety in 1953, studying a map of Tokyo and contemplating what it would take to give the Gospel to every family in that city as well as the whole nation of Japan, it was clear that prayer was essential. The 29-year-old visionary flew home from that ministry trip convinced God had shown him the key to accomplishing this every-home vision, not just in Japan but in the whole world: continuous prayer.

Within days of his return, Jack began mobilizing believers to contribute not just dollars for desperately needed literature, but one or more quarter-hours every day to pray for world evangelization. There are, Jack pointed out, 96 fifteen-minute periods in every day. The average person sleeps about 32 of these (or eight hours), and many work an additional 32. Then Jack would ask, "What are you doing with your remaining 32 fifteen-minute time periods?"

McAlister devoted a substantial amount of time on his radio program to prayer mobilization, and did so for more than three decades of regular broadcasting. He devoted two full months a year, January and June, exclusively to mobilizing prayer (instead of money) for missions.

In one remarkable step of faith in the late 1970s, Jack produced a five-hour television program, telethon-style, titled "Change the World." Its exclusive purpose: to mobilize people to give fifteen minutes every day in prayer for a lost world. By that time more than two hundred million quarter-hours of prayer had been mobilized for missions. But through the telecast, which was aired for a year in almost every television market in America, Canada and Australia, double that amount was mobilized![2]

It was during these days that I joined the staff of Every Home for Christ as the director of prayer mobilization. At the heart of my role with EHC was to develop a multihour prayer training seminar called the Change the World School of Prayer. Over the three decades that have followed more than two million believers from some 120 countries have been challenged in the School of Prayer to cultivate a daily prayer encounter with a harvest focus. Today the training has been revised and updated in an all-new format particularly designed for small groups, families and individuals who want to grow in prayer.

Links toward Completion

To continue this prayer and evangelism heritage, Every Home for Christ built a beautiful headquarters facility in Colorado Springs, Colorado, called The Jericho Center for Global Evangelism. The Jericho Center motto is: "Where Christ's Body unites, walls fall!"

Labeled The Jericho Center because of the twelve tribes of Israel coming together in unity under the banner of a God-given strategy (Joshua 5:13–6:5), this unique center not only houses EHC's international headquarters but several other global networking ministry strategies. The Jericho Center has state-of-the-art facilities to host consultations that seek to unite many evangelism and discipleship efforts committed to help complete the Great Commission. Saturated with on-site prayer and worship—in rooms designated specifically for this purpose—regular consultations are conducted, linking four components. These links include:

1. The Planning Link—Consultations that seek to unite ministries that do research necessary to plan what is needed to develop a unified strategic plan for a specific project, nation or region of the world.
2. The Equipping Link—Consultations, after the planning process, that seek to link many like-minded organizations with a gifting or calling to equip ministries who may wish to be involved in the project targeted.
3. The Going Link—Consultations that are (or desire to be) directly involved in participating "on the ground" to help carry out the project or region targeted for a unified evangelism strategy.
4. The Discipling Link—Consultations that bring together ministries uniquely gifted and committed to following-up and discipling the fruit (souls!) resulting from all that has transpired in a specific project evolved through these four links.

One such consultation process that began in 2006 targeted an entire province in Ethiopia, North Africa, for church planting. A two-year period resulted in 1,413 new churches being planted and 55,000 new believers being baptized. These congregations have now committed themselves to visit every home in their province and plant another 1,500 new fellowships over a three-year period. This would mean almost every village and town in the province would have its own church. To me there is little doubt that this Ethiopian advance and the extraordinary fruit produced was the result of a God-saturated strategy born out of prayer.

Harvest Transformation

I've seen with my own eyes other tangible evidence that God-saturated strategies (those born out of and sustained in worship and prayer) are the strategies that produce the most lasting fruit. They also anoint, sustain and protect the workers involved in carrying out these strategies, often in very hostile areas.

Take the significant upheaval that took place in Nepal during the early 1980s and the harvest transformation that followed. During this time as many as two hundred Christians were jailed for three to seven years for their evangelistic activities, while EHC workers continued providing the Gospel to as many as thirty thousand families every month—systematically, house to house. Not a single worker was detained for more than a few hours, let alone convicted or sentenced to prison. And during those years of village outreach, more than fifty thousand written response cards requesting Bible study lessons were received at various post office boxes (which were often changed for security reasons) in Kathmandu.

After democratic reforms came to Nepal in the early 1990s, I traveled to that Himalayan nation to see the work firsthand. I asked our EHC director there if he had an explanation as to why so many workers had escaped detection, and what he felt accounted for the amazing results, including the planting of more than 1,500 village house churches (which today have multiplied to more than eight thousand). He was convinced, he told me, that these blessings had resulted from prayer.

Just after his own conversion to Christ during severe days of persecution in the 1970s, he had heard that perhaps forty or fifty years earlier, believers in India (including Nepalese Christians living in India) had stood in long lines shoulder to shoulder along the India-Nepal border, facing Nepal and praying for the salvation of Nepal's people.

Our Nepalese director was convinced that when the every-home campaign was launched in Nepal in 1983 during difficult times, God was honoring all those prayers, including the tens of millions of quarter-hours of prayer EHC had mobilized outside Nepal.

One way God did this, our director told me, was by keeping the workers safe. Another way was by giving them unique ideas on how to go about their house-to-house campaign.

Since the government approved of using literature as a means to teach proper hygiene in Nepalese villages, for example, the Holy Spirit whispered to the director's heart the idea of developing a small booklet explaining the importance of health and hygiene.

The booklet gave many suggestions contributing to good health. It included illustrations about how to kill germs and even how to build an outdoor latrine. Then it warned of enemies of the spirit and soul—invisible poisons that cannot be seen or washed away by normal means. It spoke openly of the greatest enemy of our lives, Satan, who seeks to destroy our souls and lead us to an eternity of pain and suffering in a place called hell. The only cure for Satan's scheme, the booklet explained, is knowing and trusting the Creator of the universe, the one true God, who sent His only Son, Jesus Christ, to make possible the ultimate cleansing of the soul.

The booklet concluded with a simple presentation of the Gospel in terms the average Hindu could comprehend, so that every reader could learn how to repent of sin, trust in Christ and become His true follower.

What a creative way to present the Gospel legally in that nation! Our Nepalese director knew the idea had come from God and that the booklet easily gained the approval of the censors because so much prayer had covered the project.

But now the workers had to deal with Nepal's law forbidding the open distribution of Christian literature. The law did not permit "free" distribution of religious propaganda, so EHC workers began going house to house selling these booklets on hygiene (physical and spiritual) at a price so ridiculously low—a little more than a U.S. penny—that anyone could afford to buy one. For those who lacked even that tiny sum, the Christian workers would say, "Please take a copy anyway; others have given enough extra, so it's already paid for"—which was true, because when many Christians in Nepal heard about the campaign, they gave extra gifts to help.

According to the Nepal EHC director, not one worker could remember a single person refusing a booklet. Before long thousands of requests for further information on how to overcome "the great Satan" came in to Every Home Nepal's various post office boxes in Kathmandu.

Today, more than ten years later, the law permits use of a much wider range of Christian literature and follow-up materials, and the number of response cards that have been received at the EHC office in Kathmandu has now exceeded three hundred thousand. The director there does not know the nameless saints who have prayed so passionately for Nepal, but he does know their prayers are responsible for the remarkable harvest.

The Harvest Warrior

The fate of the world lies not only in the hands of nameless saints who pray, but in the hands of those like F. C. Case who give sacrificially even as they pray. I call these saints harvest warriors, because they war for the harvest through both praying and giving.

Charles and Lettie Cowman, founders of the Oriental Missionary Society, were two such harvest warriors. They had gone to Japan in the early 1900s to launch what they called the "Every Creature Crusade." Lettie later would become famous for compiling the timeless devotional classic *Streams in the Desert*. In Charles's last message in 1900 before leaving the United States for Japan, he spoke of what had driven him and Lettie to make the decision to go to Japan:

> Some years ago I read a book entitled *Dawn on the Hills of Tang*. It said, "The investment of life is the most momentous of all human decisions." The investment of influence gave me a larger vision, that it is not a light thing to live out a whole human life and to live it in such a way as to bring large returns. The paramount question that towers above every other, at whatever point we may have reached, is: "How can I now invest the rest of my life so it will bring the largest return?"[3]

Lettie Cowman never forgot those words, even long after Charles died in 1924 and she was left with the task of carrying on the vision for the "Every Creature Crusade" that had been conducted in Japan.

She liked to recall an experience that happened on a wintry December afternoon in 1932 during the height of the Great Depression. Funds had become so scarce that the Koreans serving with the Oriental Missionary Society were informed at their yearly convention that the 24 new graduates of the Bible Training Institute who had expected to open new missions would be unable to do so. It seemed the enemy of their souls was sitting directly beside the empty treasury, Lettie wrote later, and telling her, "Now the work will fail!"

But the students at the convention began to pray fervently. They sang and shouted with voices of triumph. They seemed to sense the answer was on its way.

Then, according to Lettie, out of their deep poverty many Korean Christians of the surrounding area came and placed their gifts into the offering plate. It soon became too small to hold all the sacrifices. Although the weather outside was freezing cold, men took off their overcoats and placed them in the offering. They gave leather shoes, watches, briefcases, eyeglasses and blankets. Women took silver pins from their hair and put them in the offering. No one was coaxing them on but the Holy Spirit. One small Korean woman, whose mission station was located high in the mountains 340 miles away, walked down the aisle and placed her return railway ticket into the offering plate. She said she would walk home.

According to Mrs. Cowman, this giving meeting began at two in the afternoon and continued until ten that night, when a missionary whose heart was full of emotion went to the platform and commanded them to give no more. "I can bear it no longer," he said.

After that meeting, all the workers returned to their stations. The sacrifices were converted into cash, and the amount received was nearly $3,500 (a sum that today would be twenty times that amount). The 24 new graduates had exactly enough to make it to their pioneer assignments far inland, as planned. God had supplied every need.[4]

The Money Box

I believe the fate of the world today depends on this kind of a sacrificial spirit. It is reported that Christians worldwide have a total annual personal income of approximately eight trillion dollars. The same Christians, it is estimated, give only 1.5 percent annually—less than a sixth of a tithe—to all aspects of church ministry, both locally and nationally. And only a meager 0.1 percent goes to foreign missions—about a tenth of a penny out of every dollar.[5] The resources to evangelize the world are available if only believers will release them!

Jesus spoke frequently of the need for a right perspective on how we manage our resources. He cautioned His disciples:

> "Do not lay up for yourselves treasures on earth, where moth and rust destroy and where thieves break in and steal; but lay up for yourselves treasures in heaven, where neither moth nor rust destroys and where thieves do not break in and steal. For where your treasure is, there your heart will be also."
>
> Matthew 6:19–21, NKJV

One nameless saint in Europe took this passage to heart just a few years ago, when he thought of a special treasure he had kept for years that might help build Christ's Kingdom, if only he would release it.

This German saint, whom we will call Franz, knew about the tremendous need for Gospel messages to reach the lost in Germany and beyond, and he had long believed in the vision of Every Home for Christ globally. So he visited Jörg Enners, then-director of EHC in Germany. East and West Germany had just reunited, and the opportunities for spreading the Gospel seemed endless. But Jörg lacked even enough money to pay the monthly bills for the ministry.

Franz listened intently to the need and promised to pray.

A few days later he came back to Jörg and handed him a small metal box. It was filled with rare gold and silver coins representing his entire life savings.

"Why have you brought me these?" Jörg asked, stunned.

"I struggled with myself," Franz admitted. "But the Lord told me three times to give my collection away. So I want to give these coins to your ministry."

Jörg, amazed at the man's unselfishness, was able to sell the coins to a collector for three thousand dollars, which he promptly used to settle urgent needs for the EHC work in Germany.

But that is not the end of the story. A few weeks later Franz called Jörg to tell him he had just received a telephone call informing him that he had won second place in a special contest. The prize was worth more than four thousand dollars. Franz could not believe it—it was a thousand dollars more than the gift of coins he had given.

The story still does not end there. Shortly afterward, the man who had bought the coins from Jörg showed up at the EHC German office. Something was troubling him.

"I know someone gave you these coins so you could sell them on behalf of the ministry," he said. "But I believe God wants me to give them back to you, so you can give them back to the person who gave them to you." He added, "And you can keep the money I gave you for the coins."

When Jörg gave Franz back the coins, Franz could hardly believe it. The value of the contents of the money box, when added to the prize money he had collected, meant that God had blessed Franz's faithfulness by more than doubling his initial gift.

This would seem a fitting end to the story, had God not planned one final surprise. When Jörg told the unusual testimony of the money box in EHC's monthly newsletter for

German believers, a reader (yet another nameless saint) was so touched by the account that she sent the ministry her own money box filled with similar rare coins. Now both Franz and Every Home for Christ had been doubly blessed. And because of these sacrifices, many more could hear about Jesus.

It Must Be Done!

So where do we go from here? Nameless saints, I believe, hold in their hands the key to history's greatest harvest—a thought that leads us, as we conclude, to a vital question:

What do we do about the challenge set before us to finish the task of world evangelization?

Do we join forces with those compassionate Christians like F. C. Case, the Cowmans and the company of courageous Koreans who, in a freezing cold December, gave so much and kept so little? Or do we retreat from tangible, sacrificial involvement and bask in the comfort of a sometimes uncaring generation, too concerned with self-gratification?

One thing is certain: Someday a generation of followers of Christ will arise to finish the Commission Christ gave the Church to tell all the world of His love.

The noted evangelist D. L. Moody said of the ultimate evangelization of the world: "It can be done; it ought to be done; it must be done!"[6]

Do we really believe that? If we do, let's join the ranks of that growing army of nameless saints committed to see Christ's Kingdom come, His will be done and the whole earth filled with His glory (see Revelation 11:15; Habakkuk 2:14). Together we can finish the task!

Epilogue

A Reason to Rejoice!

Writing in his excellent and encouraging book *The Hope at Hand*, David Bryant shares so many hopeful signs of an existing and coming awakening that he finds it necessary to add several substantial appendixes to describe them. In one appendix alone, Bryant shares 83 astonishing facts he calls "encouraging highlights of world revival." In another he describes seventy additional "inspiring accounts" resulting from what he calls "distinctive praying."[1]

Bryant cites missiological research indicating that about 70 percent of all progress toward completing the Great Commission has taken place just since 1900. Of that, 70 percent has occurred since World War II. And 70 percent of that has come about since 1992.[2]

Further, it is estimated there are now more than 2,520 Christian radio and television stations around the world, providing potential access to the Gospel to 4.6 billion of the world's people—in their own languages.[3]

According to a variety of researchers, as Bryant points out, a mass movement in organized Christianity began to get underway in East Asia only around 1980. In that year there were an estimated sixteen million Christians in all of East Asia. Less than ten years later that number had grown to eighty million.[4]

Other equally inspiring testimonies offer additional hope. In Laos the Church has grown from five thousand to twenty thousand in just five years. Nagaland, India, a region that was once considered 90 percent Christian, is now claiming to be 100 percent Christian. As many as fifteen thousand Christian baptisms are believed to be occurring per week in Hindu India, and reports indicate that nearly 80 percent of these have responded to Christ through some kind of supernatural encounter.[5]

In Indonesia, the world's most populated Muslim nation (with 195,623,000 people), the percentage of Christians is so high, according to one researcher, that the government will not release accurate figures.[6]

In Mongolia as recently as 1991, there were only about fifteen known believers in the entire population of two million. Today that number is at least one thousand, with many worship places emerging in major population centers.[7]

If God has some amazing developments up His sleeves (as we observed in an opening chapter), it seems He has especially opened His sleeves over China, where between 25,000 and 35,000 Chinese are said to be coming to Christ daily. (Some believe it may be as high as 50,000 a day.) So remarkable is the harvest that accurate numbers are hard to obtain. Even the Three Self Patriotic Church Movement in China, which is government-supervised, is experiencing amazing growth. In numbers of congregations alone, it has increased from four thousand to seven thousand in just five years.[8]

And not all Three Self church groups report accurate numbers to the government, for fear of future crackdowns that might hinder their ability to function freely. I spoke with one Three Self church leader who still reports his membership to the government as 150, in spite of the fact it is now well over 1,500. If the authorities knew the real numbers, he fears, they would split up his church.

The old Soviet Union, now the Commonwealth of Independent States (CIS), has also experienced both awakening and harvest. After seventy years of oppression, according to Bryant, the Christian movement there represents an astonishing 36 percent of the population, or more than one hundred million—five times the size the Communist Party ever reached.[9]

Before 1991, Every Home for Christ had not visited a single home with the Gospel in the Soviet Union. But in the 36 months following the official breakup of the nation, with Gorbachev dissolving the USSR officially on Christmas Day 1991, EHC went freely to more than fifteen million homes and received nearly one million responses. Immediately prior to the Billy Graham crusade in Moscow in October 1992, EHC worked with 57 evangelical churches in the city to place a Gospel message and crusade invitation in almost half a million homes in central Moscow.

Africa, too, is seeing an expanding harvest. In 1900 only 4 percent of the population was estimated to be Christian. Today that figure is said to be well over 40 percent and moving rapidly toward the 50 percent mark, which may already have come. In the ministry of Every Home for Christ alone, in one recent twelve-month period, more than 750,000 Africans sent in responses—and that was only in French-speaking Africa. And in just one African country, Nigeria, in a single mass crusade sponsored jointly by both charismatic and evangelical churches, German evangelist Reinhard Bonnke spoke to crowds in excess of a million, and more than 250,000 made decisions to follow Christ in the five-night campaign.

Blessings are also pouring forth from God's sleeves over Latin America, where the evangelical movement is said to be growing three times faster than the population.[10] In an article in the *Los Angeles Times*, a Roman Catholic journalist estimated that at the present rate of conversions to evangelical Christianity in Latin America, the entire population of the region will be evangelical by the end of the twenty-first century.[11]

Students of prayer and God's Word are not surprised at the growing harvest and the miracles accompanying it. For one thing, they have been praying passionately for these developments, and they know and believe God answers prayer. Then, too, they realize Scripture speaks of end-time revival and harvest, with the ultimate result that "the earth will be full of the knowledge of the LORD as the waters cover the sea" (Isaiah 11:9).

The Accelerating Harvest

We are closer to the fulfillment of this promise than many realize. And although many ministries and denominations can attest to this reality, I share examples primarily from the outreach of Every Home for Christ because I am more aware of the results reported from our campaigns.

In less than two decades in French and Anglo-Africa, Every Home Campaigns have seen more than 53 million families visited and given the Gospel of Jesus Christ. According to the World Health Organization, about 5.2 people live in each home all over the world: that means that more than 275 million people have been given access to the Good News (within hand's reach) in French and Anglo-Africa in some two decades.

The written responses in French Africa to the printed Gospel messages (in the form of mailed decision cards to African offices), as well as verbal decisions by illiterate peoples as recorded by field evangelists, are especially encouraging. Well over 4.6 million "Decision for Jesus" response cards, as well as registered reports of people praying to receive Jesus, have been processed in this region alone. One-third of this total, remarkably, came during just one twelve-month period, further indicating both the acceleration of the harvest and the amazing receptivity of those receiving the message.

In South Asia, which includes EHC's outreaches in Sri Lanka, Nepal, Bhutan, Bangladesh and the vast nation of India, the results are equally encouraging. Since 1964 more than 528,218,281 Gospel messages have been hand-delivered house to house, each with a decision card. Because two Gospel booklets, one for adults and one for children, are usually delivered to each home, it means that these booklets have touched more than 250 million families throughout the region.

In India alone, 8,627,497 written decision cards have been processed in the last four decades. In Nepal more than 335,782 decision cards have been received since the campaign began in 1983. In addition, more than 8,400 Christ Groups (house churches) have been formed by Every Home for Christ in Nepal, including many hundreds in isolated villages scattered in the Himalayan mountains. EHC Bible course graduates now can be found in nine thousand villages of Nepal.

In Bangladesh, a strictly Islamic nation of 132.3 million people, about 42 million inhabitants representing more than eight million families have already been given the Good News personally at their homes, and 245,047 people (an amazing figure for a Muslim land) have responded in writing by sending a decision card to EHC's Bangladesh office. These inquirers have been sent a simple but effective four-part Bible correspondence course.

In East Asia, including Indonesia, Malaysia, Thailand, Korea, Singapore and Japan, more than 453,813,521 Gospel messages have been hand-delivered to an estimated two hundred million families. And in spite of the strong influence of religions like Islam, Hinduism and Buddhism, 2,006,130 decision cards have been followed up with Bible lessons as of May 2008. Most of this has occurred in less than 35 years, further suggesting that God does indeed have something special up His sleeves regarding the ultimate completion of the Great Commission.

Even in Myanmar, where Adoniram Judson preached two centuries ago, 29,086 people have now responded to Gospel messages, including at least one hundred Buddhist monks, more than thirty of whom have been so transformed that they are now themselves giving the Gospel house to house! Again, most of this has happened in less than a decade.

Latin America has also been touched dramatically by the every home strategy. More than 480 million Gospel messages in Spanish, as well as other tribal dialects, have been delivered, most of them home by home, throughout all of Latin America. As of this writing, more than 2,940,000 decision cards have been received and processed as a result.

Work is presently underway to take a witness of the Gospel, as well as the love of Christ through humanitarian assistance, to the estimated seventeen million children living in the streets and alleys of Latin American cities. Instead of calling this an Every Home Crusade, organizers are labeling the effort an "Every Street Crusade," since these youngsters literally live in the streets, alleys, parks, dumps and even sewers.

In Europe, in spite of the sometimes lukewarm attitude of churches toward evangelistic endeavors, more than 326,013,701 printed messages about Christ have been delivered systematically by many hundreds of churches to more than one hundred million families in twenty nations. More than 942,269 Europeans have responded in writing to testify that they have been touched by the Gospel message and want to receive further Bible instruction.

In the CIS and Eastern Europe, almost thirty million families have been visited and given the Good News of Jesus Christ just in the decade of the 1990s. Based on the World Health Organization's global estimate of 5.2 people per home, this means as many as 156 million people in the region have been exposed to the Gospel—within hand's reach, in their homes. And for the vast majority, it was their first encounter with the Gospel.

Already nearly one million people throughout what is now called Eurasia have indicated in writing that they have prayed to receive Christ as Savior or that they want additional materials about Jesus. And because often it is only one person from a family who responds, it is possible that the actual number coming to Christ is considerably higher.

Smaller regions of the world are being affected in a similar way. Although the islands of the Pacific represent considerably smaller populations than those on the continents, the per capita response to house-to-house evangelism is sometimes double or triple that of other regions of the world. In the Pacific, for example, almost 10 percent of the Gospel booklets distributed throughout some three hundred islands have resulted in decision cards coming to the EHC offices in the region—or 112,224 decision cards in response to a systematic, home-to-home distribution of 1,950,461 evangelistic messages. And most of this has happened in only two decades.

A further indication of the acceleration of the harvest in recent years is the unusual percentage of increases of people responding to Christ, as compared to similar outreaches only a few years ago. In 1989, for example, in response to EHC's house-to-house evangelism, just over 342,000 people sent in decision cards to our offices throughout the world. This represented approximately nine hundred decision cards per day. By 1992 that number had increased to 426,031—an encouraging 25 percent increase, but not overwhelming. By the year 2000 the number was more than 756,000. Since then the responses have increased even more remarkably. In 2007, follow-up courses going to new believers or those responding to the Gospel through EHC campaigns reached 8,400,000. This represents an average of over 23,000 per day. Again, other ministries could share similar increases.

There is little doubt that the Church is moving rapidly toward that grand event when the seventh angel will blow his trumpet and heavenly voices will declare, "The kingdom of the world has become the kingdom of our Lord and of his Christ" (Revelation 11:15). That is God's epilogue on the history of humankind. And we have reason to rejoice that He is quite possibly writing its final chapter, even in this moment!

But He wants to use you and me to join Him in helping make this happen. May we be a glorious part of the divine narrative of signs and wonders and remarkable harvest advances that mark the culmination of this present age.

Notes

Chapter 2 Mountains of Mystery

1. Edgardo Silvoso, *That None Should Perish* (Ventura, Calif.: Regal, 1994), 128.

Chapter 3 People of the Trees

1. Richard Preston, *The Hot Zone* (New York: Anchor Books, 1995), 105–8.
2. Douglas H. Chadwick, "Ndoki—Last Place on Earth," *National Geographic*, July 1995, 45.

Chapter 4 Back in Fashion

1. Frank Kaleb Jansen, "When Theology, Missiology and Futurology Clash," *International Journal of Frontier Missions*, January–March 1995, vol. 12:1, 3–6.
2. W. E. Vine, *An Expository Dictionary of New Testament Words* (Old Tappan, N.J.: Revell, 1966), 228.
3. Silvoso, 60.
4. Jack McAlister, *Alaska: Assignment Accomplished* (Studio City, Calif.: World Literature Crusade, 1960), 51.
5. S. D. Gordon, *What It Will Take to Change the World* (Grand Rapids: Baker, 1979), 41–42.

Chapter 5 Seeds of the Harvest

1. Lettie Cowman, *Missionary Warrior: Charles E. Cowman* (Greenwood, Ind.: OMS International, 1989), 34.
2. *USA Today*, September 8, 1995, 1.

3. Patrick Johnstone, *Operation World* (Bromley, Kent.: STL Books, 1986), 467.

4. H. Osberg and J. Hoagland, *Attempt the Impossible* (Studio City, Calif.: World Literature Crusade, 1968), 23.

5. Yohann Lee, *Dawn of a New Era* (Studio City, Calif.: World Literature Crusade, 1962), 47.

6. Ibid., 29.

7. Robert G. Lee, *Everybody* magazine, World Literature Crusade, vol. 1, no. 2, 1969, 16.

Chapter 8 Graveyard of Siberia

1. Jim Montgomery, *DAWN 2010: A Strategy for the End of the Age* (Orlando, Fla.: DAWN Ministries, n.d.), 14.

Chapter 10 Warriors of the Night

1. It is unfortunate that for security purposes it is necessary to change our brother's name (as well as some other names throughout this book). In time I believe it will be possible to acknowledge this quality servant of the Lord whose heart beats passionately for the lost of China. Pray for Brother Fu. God knows who he is.

Chapter 11 Cords of Completion

1. Todd Johnson and Ralph Winter, "Will We Fail Again?" a compilation of previously printed works edited by Rick Wood, *Mission Frontiers* bulletin (Pasadena: U.S. Center for World Mission, July/August 1993), 12.

2. Ibid.

3. David Bryant, *The Hope at Hand* (Grand Rapids: Baker, 1995), 31.

4. Ibid.

5. Ibid., 222.

6. Ibid.

Chapter 12 The Fate of the World

1. Paul E. Billheimer, *Destined for the Throne* (Fort Washington, Pa.: Christian Literature Crusade, 1975), 106.

2. During those days I joined with the ministry of Every Home for Christ to develop the Change the World School of Prayer, which has taught more than two million believers globally to change the world through their prayers. For information on the Change the World School of Prayer DVD course for churches and individuals, write Every Home for Christ, P.O. Box 64000, Colorado Springs, CO 80962.

3. Cowman, 47.

4. Ibid., 158–59.

5. Bryant, 225.

6. D. L. Moody, quoted in *A.D. 2000 & Beyond Handbook,* Luis Bush, ed. (Colorado Springs: A.D. 2000 & Beyond, 1993), 3.

Epilogue: A Reason to Rejoice!

1. Bryant, 231.
2. Ibid., 221.
3. Ibid., 222.
4. Ibid., 223.
5. Ibid., 224.
6. Ibid.
7. Ibid., 225.
8. Ibid.
9. Ibid.
10. Ibid., 227.
11. Richard Rodriguez, "Latin Americans Convert from Catholicism to a More Private Protestant Belief," *Los Angeles Times*, August 13, 1989, Opinion Section, 1.

Index

Uchida, 135

Vine, W. E., 68

World Conquest (O. Smith), 87
World Evangelical Alliance, 163
World Literature Crusade, 76

Yambuku Mission Hospital, 48

Zaire (Democratic Republic of Congo),
48–49, 51
Zhitomir, 119–20

About the Author

Dick Eastman serves as International President of Every Home for Christ (EHC), a ministry committed to taking a printed presentation of the Gospel of Jesus Christ to every home on earth, systematically. To date, Every Home Campaigns have been conducted in 198 nations. With a full-time staff of more than 4,000 worldwide and a volunteer force exceeding 15,000 during any given month, EHC workers visit an average of 175,000 families every day, following up more than 20,000 decisions and responses daily. To date, more than 2.6 billion Gospel messages have been distributed worldwide through Every Home for Christ, resulting in over 60 million decisions and responses.

Dick is also the author of more than fifteen books on prayer, evangelism and Christian growth with three million copies in print. Since 1992, Dick has also served as president of America's National Prayer Committee, providing oversight to the planning of America's annual National Day of Prayer, the first Thursday of May. Dick's wife, Dee, is active in Dick's ministry, annually traveling with him more than four times around the world.

About Every Home for Christ

Every Home for Christ has faithfully served the body of Christ globally for more than half a century. If you would like to be involved in partnering with Every Home for Christ to spread the Gospel globally, home by home, visit the EHC website at www.ehc.org. You may also contact the Every Home for Christ office at 640 Chapel Hills Rd., Colorado Springs, CO 80920, or call 1-800-423-5054.

You can be involved in helping spread the Gospel globally through Every Home for Christ by committing to pray daily and then by giving generously as God enables you. To help you pray more meaningfully, you can also request a copy of a full-color World Prayer Map from the EHC office nearest to you.

EHC's History at a Glance

The ministry of Every Home for Christ began in Canada in 1946.

The first Every Home Campaign involving systematic home-by-home evangelism began in Japan in 1953.

There have been campaigns conducted in 198 nations, with complete coverage in 101 nations.

More than 2.6 billion Gospel booklets and face-to-face contacts have been made, resulting in over 60 million followed-up decision cards and responses.

Decisions/responses are followed up with Bible lessons. Where there are no churches, Christ Group fellowships are planted. To date, more than 112,000 Christ Groups have been formed.

In a recent twelve-month period, 144,000 homes (an estimated 720,000 people) were reached per day, and an average of 13,995 responses per day received follow-up from EHC.

More than 19,000 workers worldwide are involved with EHC in any given month, of which 75 percent are volunteers.

Your Invitation to Visit the Watchman Wall and Training Center

The Jericho Center for Global Evangelism, Colorado Springs, Colorado

The Jericho Center for Global Evangelism in Colorado Springs, Colorado, is the international headquarters of Every Home for Christ (EHC), and is also home to numerous other ministries similarly focused on completing the Great Commission. It now also houses an 8,000-square-foot area dedicated to mobilizing and training strategic prayer for harvest advances throughout the world, equipping and inspiring intercessors while simultaneously providing space for ongoing (24/7) intensive prayer and intercessory worship. Included in this area is a 500-seat Watchman Training Center as well as a unique "prayer wall" patterned after the ancient Wailing Wall in Jerusalem. This wall, constructed with fifty tons of actual Jerusalem stone from a quarry where stone came for the original Western Wall, was completed in April 2009.

Serving as a visual symbol of "watchmen on the wall" (see Isaiah 62:6–7) who pray day and night without ceasing, this unique wall also serves as a headquarters for mobilizing continual prayer for all the nations of the world, recruiting believers globally to find their place on a "wall of prayer" in their area. (A "wall of prayer" consists of all 168 hours in a week filled with committed intercessors who are agreeing in prayer over specific focuses for the nations or their geographic area.) The ultimate goal of the Watchman Training Center is to fill every moment of every day—in every time zone and major city of the world—with focused intercession and worship for global awakening. Additionally, EHC's "wall of prayer" includes thirteen individual "prayer grottos" (rooms) for intercessors who wish to spend whole or half days in intensive intercession for the nations. Twelve of these rooms are named after the tribes of Israel and the remaining grotto is called "The Back to Jerusalem Room" to highlight the Chinese Church's vision to someday send tens of thousands of Christian missionaries along the old silk roads through Central Asia and the Middle East—all the way back to Jerusalem.

This area of the Jericho Center also houses an auditorium for up to five hundred participants. This allows EHC the flexibility to host larger consultations and prayer training events. Room dividers further allow the auditorium to be divided into three separate areas to accommodate several simultaneous training efforts or consultations for various-sized groups. This training area is used to inspire, train and mobilize believers in strategic prayer and intercessory worship as well as to provide space for hosting consultations related to united global evangelism and discipleship projects. With state-of-the-art media technology in this new area, EHC and other partner ministries are also able to broadcast live training sessions globally or record sessions for webcasting and other distribution means, thereby maximizing the training's availability to a much wider global audience.